BEST BOSS EVER

An Insider's Guide to Modern People Management

BEST BOSS EVER

An Insider's Guide to Modern People Management

Kris Dunn

Society for Human Resource Management
Alexandria, Virginia www.shrm.org
Society for Human Resource Management, India
Mumbai, India www.shrmindia.org
Society for Human Resource Management, Middle East and Africa Office
Dubai, United Arab Emirates www.shrm.org/pages/mena.aspx

This publication is designed to provide accurate and authoritative information regarding the subject matter covered. It is sold with the understanding that neither the publisher nor the author is engaged in rendering legal or other professional service. If legal advice or other expert assistance is required, the services of a competent, licensed professional should be sought. The federal and state laws discussed in this book are subject to frequent revision and interpretation by amendments or judicial revisions that may significantly affect employer or employee rights and obligations. Readers are encouraged to seek legal counsel regarding specific policies and practices in their organizations.

This book is published by SHRM. The interpretations, conclusions, and recommendations in this book are those of the author and do not necessarily represent those of the publisher.

SHRM books and products are available on most online bookstores and through the SHRMStore at shrmstore.org.

SHRM creates better workplaces where employers and employees thrive together. As the voice of all things work, workers and the workplace, SHRM is the foremost expert, convener and thought leader on issues impacting today's evolving workplaces. With nearly 325,000 members in 165 countries, SHRM impacts the lives of more than 235 million workers and families globally. Learn more at SHRM.org.

Library of Congress Cataloging-in-Publication Data

Names: Dunn, Kris, author.

Title: Best boss ever : an insider's guide to modern people management / Kris Dunn.
Description: Alexandria, Virginia : Society for Human Resource Management, [2023] | Includes bibliographical references. | Summary: "Tools and best practices to help those who manage teams lead with greater impact and effectiveness"-- Provided by publisher.
Identifiers: LCCN 2022017004 (print) | LCCN 2022017005 (ebook) | ISBN 9781586445362 (paperback) | ISBN 9781586445416 (pdf) | ISBN 9781586445461 (epub) | ISBN 9781586445515 (mobi)
Subjects: LCSH: Executive ability. | Teams in the workplace--Management. | Leadership. | Organizational behavior.
Classification: LCC HD38.2 .D865 2023 (print) | LCC HD38.2 (ebook) | DDC 658.4/092--dc23/eng/20220408

Printed in the United States of America   FIRST EDITION

PB Printing

10 9 8 7 6 5 4 3 2 1   SKU: 61.19301

Contents

PART III

OTHER STUFF WE SHOULD TALK ABOUT

PART IV

WINNING

PART V

BUILD IT AND THEY WILL COME

Foreword

Kris Dunn Is My Best Friend, and There's Nothing Weird about That

Kris Dunn and I are best friends. Wow, that's a big statement, one you rarely see a grown man make! I mean, I've been a dude my entire life, and I think I would rather drink gasoline than admit another man is my best friend, unless I've been out drinking. Then every dude will tell you that you're his best friend!

When you are best friends with someone, it means that you know them as well as they know themselves. The most famous thing about Kris Dunn is he played college basketball with the professional wrestler Kane (WWE brother of The Undertaker for the uninitiated). Glenn Jacobs is his real name, and he was the best man at KD's wedding. Yeah, I call him "KD" because that's what best friends do.

Why wasn't I the best man? Great question. KD and I didn't meet until we were already far into our professional careers. Otherwise, in a do-over, I'm certainly riding shotgun on the wedding bus!

The world of work is filled with epic best friend working tandems. You have Turk and JD (Zach Braff and Donald Faison) from *Scrubs*. Snoop Dog and Martha Stewart are an amazing, unlikely talent pairing, as are Amy Poehler and Tina Fey from *Saturday Night Live*. Dwayne Johnson and Kevin Hart are most like KD and me as a physical representation of best friend working tandems. Each member in these duos brings something special to the table to make the magic happen.

In my case, I bring to KD something similar to what Stacey King brought to the greatest basketball player of all time, Michael Jordan, when they played together on the Chicago Bulls. Stacey

King has a famous quote: "I will always remember this as the night that Michael Jordan and I combined to score seventy points." That night Michael scored sixty-nine points, and Stacey scored one!

I'm KD's Stacey King.

Managing a Team Is Hard: KD Can Help You Be Better

Have I ever had a Best Boss Ever? That's a great question.

I've had some good bosses for sure, but that title is probably a stretch for what they delivered. The bosses in my life all seem to just stay out of the firing line most of the time, which means survival must be a trait of a good boss, right? Part of survival in corporate life is avoiding conflict, but the truly great bosses don't run from the fight. The best bosses figure out a way to engage without getting scarred.

One of the things I've always liked about KD is he can tell you that you suck, but you don't end up hating him. Great bosses have a way of doing that. When I first started writing for *Fistful of Talent*, he always made me feel like my stuff was great—as he was asking permission to change it and publish it on a day fewer people were reading. He cared enough about me to put me in a low-volume audience spot so I would be less embarrassed and made me feel great while he was doing it! That's a great boss.

Great bosses help you be your best and, at the same time, protect you from yourself and the organization at large. What great bosses know is that once you wear that scarlet letter of *low performer* within any organization, you'll never lose that label. So the best ones will find ways to cover up your weaknesses until you figure it out and do better. So, yeah, what I'm saying is KD is like a warm, expensive hoodie in the cold corporate abyss.

Leading people and managing their performance is hard work. Don't let anyone tell you it's not. I wish I'd had all of the gold KD is rolling out in this book when I was entering corporate America and being mistaken for early Ron Howard (more specifically Richie Cunningham from *Happy Days*) or a young Michael J. Fox (aka Brantley Foster in *The Secret of My Success*).

Looking like Richie or Brantley as you try to lead your first team isn't the picture of leadership you see when you pull up the *Harvard Business Review*. This book would have helped.

Buckle Up Because This Book Starts Off with a Warning

Here's what I truly know about KD. He's a writer. He's a lot of other things, but at his core, the dude can flat-out just write. It's not an easy skill to be a writer who can educate and entertain. What most people don't know is that for over a decade, KD wrote every single day on his blog *The HR Capitalist* while he pursued a full-time career in HR and talent acquisition. As a friendly challenge, he got me to write every day on my blog as well, and it changed my life for the better.

Legendary sportswriter Red Smith was once asked what it was like having to write a column every day. The demands of it! The stress of it! Did it become a chore? His response: "Why, no," deadpanned Red. "You simply sit down at the typewriter, open your veins, and bleed." KD bleeds for you in this book.

Best Boss Ever starts out with a couple of warnings. I'll let KD share his warning soon, but here's my warning when it comes to being a great leader and manager.

Consistency can be overrated. I'm a big Michigan State Basketball fan. I love MSU's hall-of-fame coach, Tom Izzo. What makes Izzo great is that for decades, he's been super consistent in how he coaches. He demands effort, and you have to play defense. If you come to play at Michigan State and you decide those two things aren't important to you, you will not play and will most likely transfer. Forced or positive turnover is what we call that in the HR game.

But the leadership KD talks about in this book has some major differences from sports. In a corporate setting, I've found that the best leaders of people don't treat everyone the same. The conventional wisdom of "Have one leadership style, be consistent, and you'll have the best results" is mostly the stuff of average leaders.

Great bosses and great leaders adapt to the team they have. Business leaders (that's you) have imperfect information when hiring and end up with teams mixed with all kinds of talent and levels of performance. But it's your job to make it work.

The greatest bosses in the world find specific ways to get the most out of each person on their team. KD wrote you a book that will help you become a great boss. Turns out the key is using the same tools (consistency) but being mature enough to know that each conversation is going to be different (agility, customization) and it's more about them (individual team members) than you (the boss).

It won't be easy, but it'll be worth it. KD makes it palatable with hundreds of pop culture and business references delivered through quotes, metaphors, and yes, even incredibly jaded footnotes.

Seems like a perfect foreword. I got to talk about my best friend, I got to talk about myself, and I got to talk about Tom Izzo! Win-win.

—Tim Sackett, SHRM-SCP
HR Tech Authority

The Best Boss Ever Tool Kit

Within the pages of this book are tools—the best practices I've learned that have the highest degree of impact and effectiveness for those who manage teams.

When in doubt, pull this book off the shelf and use this supplemental table of contents to find the specific work-life hack you need (individual tools numbered in ascending order as they appear in this book), as well as a one-page cheat sheet at the end of skill-based chapters providing an overall refresher on core concepts.

You got this. Go show them how to lead.

Performance Management (Chapter 13)

Tool 21: How to Collect Performance Info throughout the Year

Tool 22: How to Determine the Right Performance Rating in Any Area

Tool 23: How to Write Performance Reviews That Don't Suck

Performance Management Reviews Cheat Sheet and Resources

One-on-One Meetings (Chapter 14)

Tool 24: How to Set the Right 1:1 Expectation and Vibe With Your Employees

Tool 25: The Perfect 1:1 Agenda and Flow

1:1 Meetings with Direct Reports Cheat Sheet and Resources

Recognition (Chapter 15)

Tool 26: A Checklist of Where to Use Real Time/Organic Recognition

Tool 27: How to Add Spice to Your Recognition for Greater Meaning

Recognition Cheat Sheet and Resources

WIIFM (What's In It For Me?) (Chapter 16)

Tool 28: Places to Insert WIIFM into Conversations with Employees

Tool 29: How to Transfer the WIIFM Burden on Sucky McSh*tty Activities to the Employee

WIIFM Cheat Sheet and Resources

Building Portfolios (Chapter 17)

Tool 30: The List of Things Employees Should Include in Their Portfolios

Warning

The surgeon general of rock warns that viewing
this band is equal to twenty-nine espressos.[1]
Here they are, Tenacious D!
—Open mic night MC introducing Tenacious D
to an unenthusiastic bar crowd

Not everyone is going to dig this book.

While this is a book about leadership and managing people, it does not suggest that you apply the same techniques to all the people on your team. Instead, I'm going to suggest that you segment your team as ruthlessly as Lululemon analyzes who will spend $150 for a pair of pants.

Let's face it—the Lululemon brand isn't for everyone. It's the same with interacting with your team. One size (or approach) doesn't fit all.

I wrote this book for you. Whether you're a new manager of people or a long-time leader, everyone has something they can add to their game.

I didn't write this book because I'm an expert. In many ways I am, but in other ways I'm just like you.

I've had my share of wins as a manager of people. I've had some Ls along the way as well.

The thing that makes me different is simple to spot. In 2012, I started a passion project called the *Boss Leadership Series*—a seven-module training series to provide leadership skills for the modern manager of people.

---

1. Not exactly what Jack Black wrote but edited to avoid the "R" rating right out of the gate. Look it up.

Since starting the *Boss Leadership Series*, I've served thousands of people leading teams in live and virtual training. They hate to role-play just like you do, by the way.

This book is the equivalent of a secret transcript of those leadership training sessions merged with what I've learned in a career serving leaders as the corporate version of The Wolf from *Pulp Fiction*.

Names have been changed to protect the jaded and guilty as well as the incredibly effective leaders I've learned from who wish to remain anonymous.

Your job as you read this book is to put some of the tools to work and not suck. LFG.

Part I

Forget Everything You Know

1

Origin Story: Vader

Say your prayers little one
Don't forget my son
To include everyone.
—Metallica, "Enter Sandman"

A long time ago, in a corporate office park far away, people used to be a little harsher.

Those were simpler times, my friends, before Twitter accounts and quasi "news" organizations emerged to publish a petition from 13 employees (out of **30,000**) at your company and call it evidence of the "toxic culture" at your organization.

But if we're honest with ourselves, the high performers in our midst have always required an explanation that transcends "shut up" and "do it because I said so."

Story time. Gather round the campfire, boys and girls.

"Kris? Please hold for Mr. Andrews (Vader)."

Flashback two decades ago, where a younger version of KD (that's me) is waiting to talk to the Darth Vader of HR at the Fortune 500 where I was employed.

Most people get nervous when Vader is getting ready to jump on the horn and tear things up. I was calm.

I had a lot to be cocky about. I was on some "40 under 40" list (HIPO[1] program, no big deal) and had recently been tagged to ponder a promotion to another company inside the DeathStar.com family. The portfolio company in question was struggling with people

---

1. HIPO = High Potential Employee, generally part of a formal succession plan. I knew because I was in HR. Duh.

issues, and Vader himself (probably six levels above me) plucked me off the HIPO list and shipped me off to Tatooine (actually Orlando) to interview for my first director role and survey the scene.

As I waited for Vader, I thought about the relocation. I was two trips into the evaluation: first to interview (offer extended) and second to pitch Orlando to my wife (approval granted).[2]

There was only one hitch. I was underwater related to owning a house in the new market. My calculations pointed to a $9,000 shortfall related to what I needed to stay even in level of housing versus the offer provided.

Simple, right? Logic and math. I even had a spreadsheet that I had sent him.[3] #communicator

Vader came on the phone. After exchanging pleasantries ("how's the new helmet and cape treating you," etc.), I was ready to get to business. I did a soft intro to the final issue at hand to close the deal and attempted to move to the math, at which time Vader interrupted and said the following:

> "Kris, I'm not telling you that you have to take this promotion. But if you don't, I can't guarantee you anything about the viability of your career at our company."

WTF. Spreadsheet interruptus.

Translation: "There will be no more money. Did you see what I did to the last guy who had questions? That was wild, right? Enjoy Tatooine."

Me? I accepted the threat without further attempts at negotiation and ended the call. Vader was just doing what Vader does.

---

2. We were ready to make an offer on a house in Celebration, the Disney community in Orlando. Don't judge me.
3. The spreadsheet had four rows and four columns. I was in pure beast mode. There were formulas and stuff.

I looked out the window of my office (appropriately measured for my career level by ceiling tile count[4]) and knew it was only a matter of time before I voluntarily pulled the ripcord and was gone.

It was the end of the world as I knew it, and I felt fine.

---

4. I was in a "5 wide," which was solid individual contributor status. I had that going for me, which was nice.

2

Dinosaur Crossing

*The dinosaur is having one last roar at
the meteor before it wipes him out.*
—Kendall Roy referring to his CEO father, *Succession* (HBO)

If I'm honest, I was neutral on Vader when he threw the career fastball at my head. I just knew, as a result, I wasn't taking his job, where I actually took an employee to the emergency room during my interview day (true story).[1]

Of course, he was a complete brontosaurus. But dinosaurs would dominate Class A office space for at least 15 more years until social tools like Twitter got ramped up and gave everyone a microphone and amplified something called "feelings."

Vader did fine. I'm sure he's residing in The Villages where he has access to par-3 golf and concierge healthcare.

Evolve or die when it comes to leadership. But be careful about making a stink about the old guard.

If You Come For the King, You Best Not Miss

You know the story about dinosaurs. Things were going awesome for them until it all went to hell.

Calling groups of people dinosaurs is a tricky game in the business world, primarily because the target of that moniker is usually someone in charge. You think someone's dead, and then their hand reaches up from the swamp and grabs you by the throat, and

---

1. I wanted to go on a ride-along. The dude had to climb a tree for a work-related item. Gravity won that day, friends.

suddenly you're browsing Indeed and thinking about paying someone to optimize your LinkedIn profile.

Pro tip: You've lost career traction if you're pondering the effectiveness of your "About" statement on social media.

Consider the tale of Informix, a small database company trying to mix things up in 1996.[2] Feeling frisky, Informix put up a billboard near Oracle's Redwood Shores headquarters that read: CAUTION: DINOSAUR CROSSING. Another Informix billboard on northbound Highway 101 read: YOU'VE JUST PASSED REDWOOD SHORES. SO DID WE. Oracle shot back with a billboard that implied that Informix's software was slower than snails.

Then Informix CEO Phil White decided to make things personal. When White learned that Larry Ellison enjoyed Japanese samurai culture, he commissioned a new billboard depicting the Oracle logo along with a broken samurai sword.

You can guess what happened. Informix didn't execute and was ultimately sold for parts to IBM in 2002, with Phil White spending time in a federal prison on a fraud conviction.

Larry Ellison, on the other hand, dates supermodels, buys nine-figure yachts like you and I subscribe to streaming services, and is worth 125 billion as I write this.[3]

The Old Ways That Make Our People Hate Us

It's unwise to say out loud that the old guard doesn't know what they're doing when it comes to people management. After all, they've had success and can fire you on Friday, and who can blame them for trying to add 20 percent to their retirement fund before driving their late model Cadillac into the sunset?[4]

---

2. Top Rap Song for the year—"California Love" by 2Pac. Guest appearance by future Apple Board Member, Dr. Dre.
3. If you can quote Ellison's net worth without doing the Dr. Evil pinky-to-mouth mannerism, you're better than me.
4. If I'm honest, this is a Tesla in today's world. I thought about Mazda Miata, but it didn't score well in the focus groups.

But management success that dates back to AOL email addresses and Whitesnake MTV videos isn't above critical analysis.

If we're honest with ourselves, many managers of people (including you and me) still carry some of the old ways of leadership with them as they run accounts, produce widgets, and get things done, including the following gems:

» **Making it ALL about the company.** See capitalization. *Of course*, it's about the company, until you wake up, go to therapy, and determine that every conversation you have with your people on business-related topics is about the numbers, the account that's hopelessly screwed up, and fear. There aren't any IDPs on the Death Star, storm trooper.

» **Expecting people to do things because we told them to. Sounds reasonable.** You want me to send the email to a VIP that might crush my career because—wait for it—it's good for you? Can I at least get a meaningless platitude about being a team player? No problem, I'll keep myself warm in this corporate wilderness by saving every email I've ever received[5]—just in case.

» **Demanding loyalty to the brand/organization.** It would be nice if we could talk about my career in a way that went beyond what's possible in the Pittsburgh location. That's probably not going to happen anytime soon when you appear defensive and unwilling to discuss anything cool that our competitors are doing and how we compare.

» **Not being connected to the people who work for you on a deeper level.** To be clear, I don't expect you to know what's going on with my kids these days. It would, however, be nice if you knew my general preferences at work so you could help me not get crushed by my weaknesses (I care too much) and get

---

5. My favorite name that I've heard for the CYA folder at work is "Keepers," which pretty much says it all.

me on some things that actually charge my batteries (burning Ops Manuals).

We've all got a bit of the old ways in us as managers. But some cures can be as dangerous as the condition they seek to treat.

The New Ways That Make Our People Mock Us

The old ways existed because they worked. But as new generations emerged and the social contract of working for a single company for more than five years was destroyed by outsourcing, the global economy, and resulting layoffs, the old ways worked less.

Time to pivot!

Alarmed by increased turnover and Glassdoor reviews that put companies on blast, a generation of leaders sought out the "new ways" of leadership. In embracing the "new ways," progressive leaders embraced employee autonomy, a focus on employee engagement, 360-degree feedback, and the temple of managing teams via "strengths."

While all of those items are quality adds to any leadership skill portfolio, many companies and managers went too far.

While average rank-and-file employees are happy not to be hassled for accountability, top talent in organizations secretly roll their eyes when they see the following markers of a manager taking trendy leadership theory a bit too far:

» **Constantly reading best-selling books on leadership.** I know what you're thinking. "Damn KD, isn't this a book on leadership?" Hear me out. There's nothing wrong with a manager reading books on leadership. The problem emerges when the manager reads a continuous stream of leadership books and refers to them routinely in normal conversations with their team. Dispensing advice and citing the book you heard it from doesn't make your people feel like they are dealing with "The Natural," does it?

» **Live installs of theory included in best-selling books on leadership.** That's right, I'm taking the presence of best-selling books to the graduate level. If you've ever been in a stand-up meeting at the start of your day in corporate America, someone was doing a live install of something they've read about in a leadership book. If they brought the book with them and talked about it in the stand-up meeting, the music you heard playing in the background was "Mr. Roboto" by Styx[6] (which is to say they are a little stiff and lacking human fluidity). Use the tools, but use them discreetly. It's okay to act like it's your idea; that's actually preferred.

» **Forwarding leadership skittles articles from sources like *Inc.com* and *Fast Company*.** We've all been there. Some aggregator figures out we lead people and floods us with articles on leadership/culture from a source that exists decidedly down-market from the *Harvard Business Review*. These articles, often with titles like, "LinkedIn Founder Reid Hoffman on Blitzscaling,"[7] are *leadership skittles*. Leadership skittles are defined as clickbait articles from the web that have the leadership nutritional value of the multicolored and flavored candy. Can you imagine breaking down a difficult situation with a direct report and them saying, "Hey, I was just trying to blitzscale Finance a bit on the Penske account." No? Then don't forward leadership skittles.

Let's evolve. But let's be real (read: authentic) out there, people.

---

6. A middle school teacher of mine introduced me to Styx and Queen when I was an early teenager. Is that questionable middle school teacher behavior?
7. Real title! Blitzscaling comes with counsel to "let some fires burn" and "run fast through the fog." WTF.

Merging of the Old Ways and the New
Ways Just Makes Sense

What if we didn't have to choose between the old and new ways? What if you could focus on getting things done through some of the old tools while rounding off the hard boomer-based edges via the new ways?

A mix of the two worlds is the obvious answer. After all, "discipline is the strongest form of love you can show someone."[8] Packaging that accountability in a cloak of hope and service as a manager of others is the spoonful of sugar that makes the medicine go down.

---

8. Quote from Tom Izzo, Michigan State Basketball Coach, voted by me "most likely to choke a kid out in a game."

3

Welcome to the Show, Kid

Batman doesn't do damage control. When
the sheep freeze up, you need to answer the
call and start throwing haymakers.
—Ari Gold, *Entourage*

If you're just starting your run as a manager of people, welcome to the show, kid.

Running a team will either kill you or let you live your best life. They didn't tell you that when you accepted the 16 percent raise and the office next to the close talker?[1] Shocking.

If you've had a team for a while and are tired of everyone's whining, I feel you. You've come to the right place.

We're going to teach you to play offense. But before we can do that, it's time to put you on the therapy couch, watch you curl up into the fetal position, and have a good cry.

Let's talk about you, and how you're wired in a way as a leader that routinely sees you shoot yourself in the foot. The only difference between doing that in real life versus as a manager of people is that in the corporate world, you have to make it through the Q3 budget forecast meeting before you get to go to the ER.

You Got a Team Because You Were Good at S**t

Any manager of people has a lot on their plate. After all, a general prerequisite to getting your first manager job is being an awesome

---

1. The newest manager at any location receives the worst office. Close proximity to break room/bathroom also probable.

individual contributor. Then, at some point in your first month in your new manager role, you realize(d) the reality—you still have a crap ton to do on your own as well as leading a new team.

Just because you're a manager doesn't mean you stop cranking out individual contributor greatness. You're expected to do that PLUS lead a group of people to team greatness, individual success, career fulfillment, and high-engagement survey scores as distributed by Sharon in human resources (HR).

That's why you need a plan. What type of manager do you want to be?

Inside all of us, there's a hard-wired preset—a type of manager we're most likely to be based on our behavioral DNA and the folks who have managed us in the past, etc. Who you are and how you were raised in corporate America has a lot to do with how you manage others and whether they fear you or routinely try to run you over.

And while there's undoubtedly incredible strengths in your preset as a manager, there are also things that can kill you. That's why we put together a guide for you. You can't grow unless you know what your default DNA guides you to do under pressure.

There Are Six Types of Managers of People at Your Company—You Are One of These

In my experience coaching leaders in all kinds of businesses (big and small companies alike, all industries), there are six types of managers of people that populate every organization in the world.

Grab a name tag and write your moniker in when you see it in the following list:

The Doer/Individual Contributor
This manager was a great individual contributor before they got promoted to manage people, and when the pressure hits, they revert to

what they know best: doing stuff. The Doer/Individual Contributor is excellent at what they do, and they know sometimes it's just easier for them to do it rather than train and grow their people.

Motivators: Being heads down and excellent on their own.

Turn-offs: Getting slowed down by people on their team who need <gasp> support.

Their job would be great if it wasn't for the #&#*ing people.

Left unchecked, the Doer/Individual Contributor will float through their career as a manager. They'll do what's necessary as a doer to ensure the team doesn't fail, but their results in growing great people will be spotty at best. Since they generally don't put their people in a position to fail—or succeed—their direct reports don't grow like they should. Mediocre talent finds them and never leaves.[2]

The Friend/Empathy-First/Pushover

This manager values connection and friendship above all else and is often promoted from the group they are asked to manage. That puts this manager in a tough spot—they used to be peers with the people they are now being asked to manage, and suddenly they're in a position of authority. A tough look for any new manager.

Motivators: Deep conversations with direct reports over the hum of the break room microwave.

Turn-offs: Asking a direct report where the stuff that they assigned to them is.[3]

---

2. Literally the third worst thing that can happen to you as a leader, just behind "safety liaison" and "canceled."
3. The Friend would consider promoting someone before confronting them, especially if that person was a past peer.

In addition to the "former teammate, now our manager" path, managers with low assertiveness are naturals for this persona as well. Ability to confront things needing correction is a big part of any successful manager's role, and while new managers with low assertiveness can be effective in many ways, an unwillingness to provide hard feedback and direction can limit overall effectiveness across time.

Sometimes you gotta be hard on others. The Friend/Empathy-First/Pushover has a hard time summoning that up.

The Control Freak/Authoritarian

Who's the boss? I'M THE BOSS! It's hard to fault this type of manager. After all, they were hired to get things done, and one of the best ways to get things done is to tell people what they need to do and expect it's going to happen with excellence.

> **Motivators:** Crossing off 10 things from their list. Assigning 23 other things the same day.
>
> **Turn-offs:** Direct report "feelings."

Unfortunately, growing people on your team and being a magnet for top talent doesn't happen as much as it should with the Control Freak/Authoritarian. Simply telling people what to do and barking at them when they don't get it done isn't a direct path to growth, and it doesn't create a reputation as a manager people want to work for.

Control Freaks are in danger of topping out early in their careers as managers. The higher you go, the better talent you manage, and that increasing talent level is likely to call BS on working for the drill sergeant from *Full Metal Jacket*.

Can you stop the eventual coup that's coming your way as a Control Freak? Debatable, but I'm sure force will be used early and often and without discretion!

The Trend-Spotter/Reader of Bestsellers

Mentioned earlier, the Trend-Spotter wants to be a top-tier leader—
so much so that they consume many bestsellers on their leadership
bookshelf and then the following happens:[4]

» They try to install techniques they read about in the aforementioned books without consideration to their personal style, the
needs of their team, or the existing culture.

» They reference the technique in the book, which has the unfortunate outcome of telling their team they're doing a hard install
of the technique in question.

» They do multiple installs in a given year, which gives the team
they manage the sense that—you guessed it—the ideas aren't
their own, and they install techniques without much consideration of what actually works best for the team.

Motivators: Email from Amazon announcing a new book from
Patrick Lencioni.[5]

Turn-offs: People who don't read the texts they send featuring
articles from *Fast Company.*

The Trend-Spotter's heart is in the right place, but their approach
related to reading and introducing so much external material robs
them of being viewed as authentic by their team.

The Performance Driver

The Doer and Control Freak can evolve to be a Performance Driver.
Focused clearly on organizational goals, the Performance Driver
doesn't hesitate to ask for contributions from their direct reports.

---

4. My favorite to see is *Topgrading*, an interviewing classic. Who's ready for
a four-hour interview? This guy!
5. Enter the Pavlovian response for any book featuring a number. Shout-out to
The 9 Faces of HR.

Behind every request is a simple concept—we have to do everything possible to meet our goals as a team. That positions the Performance Driver as the unemotional manager: outlining realities, measuring contributions, and asking for more.

> **Motivators:** Spreadsheets that show synergy between revenue targets and employee goals.
>
> **Turn-offs:** Reasons why things didn't get done, labeled as "excuses" on their tracker.

Team members of the Performance Driver would love to have t-shirts mocking their leader that say, "Cascade This."

While the Performance Driver is an effective manager in most organizations, it's easy for them to have one blind spot—development of their people. Agnostic calls for performance and follow-ups are often delivered with such pace that there is little time or interest left for coaching with the appropriate level of depth.

The Career Agent

Cue the heavenly music because we've arrived at the pinnacle of managing others.

The Career Agent is the fully evolved manager of people. The Career Agent approaches every conversation with a member of their team—whether assigning work, coaching performance, or providing full performance feedback—through the lens of the employee, always answering the question "what's in it for you" proactively for the employee.

> **Motivators:** People who want more for themselves.
>
> **Turn-offs:** People who just want to do the job, be left alone, and go home.

Career Agents have the ability to deliver conversations to the people they manage, in an authentic, free-flowing, believable way.

Managers with this adaptation are already thriving in today's chaotic world, and those who don't have it are struggling to keep their head above water and, at times, survive.

As you might have guessed, you can have elements of multiple personas. Doers/Individual Contributors can float into Control Freak land when they get fed up and attempt to corral the available horsepower on their team. Multiple personas drift into Trend-Spotter territory when they have momentary but fleeting focus on evolving as a manager of people.

But you're hardwired to react to pressure in a specific way as a manager of people and regression to your mean always happens. It's science.

Self-awareness is the first step toward continuous improvement.[6] Let's keep digging in.

---

6. Picture me laughing if you read this sentence and asked yourself if I stole it from another leadership book.

Bonus

Create Your Own Mission Statement on Talent for Messed Up Times

If you're like me, the pace of change in the world in the early 2020s has felt rough in a lot of ways. But like many of you, I remain incredibly blessed—I have a job, my company survived the pandemic, and my family is healthy.

But in a world with so much political and social unrest, it's easy for all of us to feel disrupted in some way. For me, all the change going on around us made me less confident to speak to many of the hard business and talent truths I have learned in my career.

You never know in today's world when you might be canceled or shamed at the drop of a hat.

The hesitation that so many people feel toward having real conversations got me thinking: *what I really needed to do was to create a mission statement of how I view people/talent issues that addresses the times and communicates what I believe.*

So I did it. I think you should do that too.

Here's my personal mission statement for who I am and what I believe my life as a leader/manager of people should be about moving forward.

> I believe every employee deserves an opportunity to earn
> a great living based on their performance. They deserve
> a safe environment that respects all people and provides
> maximum opportunity to all, regardless of race, gender,
> orientation, and any other identifier.

Of course, I'll get emails that say this isn't good enough on a variety of levels in 2023 and beyond. That's okay. I'm not writing *War and Peace* here or even a 35-page document similar to the one that got Jerry Maguire fired.[1] What's needed is a lightweight talent mission statement to keep you grounded and focused on moving forward but also allows you to call BS on things that make no sense (spoiler alert, there are a lot of that these days).

Let's break down my simple statement so I can tell you what my truth is when it comes to talent:

» **It all starts with performance wherever you are in life.** The world is a hard place, and different people have different talents, different work ethics, etc. Someone less talented needs to work harder, and many do and absolutely crush it. Some are naturally talented and skate by without putting in the hours. Put on your helmet and get ready to compete, because this world is tough. Effort, focus, and not being a victim matters.

» **There are crazy talented people from every walk of life— every race, gender, orientation, country, and any other identifier you want to name.** I know this because I've worked for them and been fortunate enough to have them on my teams during my career—from all walks of life. I want to recruit them all by the way, not because of any identifier, but because they are great at what they do. High performer and achiever is a segment that is not limited by tag, identifier, identity politics, employment law, etc. It is a DNA strand combined with grit that rises above many of the conversations we're having today.

» **The world works hard to try and lure high performers back to the pack.** There's a bunch of quotes I could give you here. Whether it's a political conversation about how the business community mistreats labor, a coworker pissed at you because you're killing it and they can't/won't, or Ricky Bobby's dad in

1. "The Things We Think and Do Not Say" from *Jerry Maguire* is a must-read for any renaissance leader. Google and enjoy.

Talladega Nights encouraging students to go fast,[2] it's noted that the world around you wants you to be average. See the first two bullet points.

» **Safety in the world—inside and outside of work—should be a given.** You should be safe in the workplace and not have to deal with BS, whether it's dealing with COVID, personal safety, or just not getting tied up with non-work-related conversations that make you feel at risk because you're not in the cool clique, etc. I want people to feel safe outside of work as well, but that's a complicated post that transcends the scope of this work mission statement.

» **Every employee and candidate deserves an environment/experience that provides maximum opportunity to all, regardless of race, gender, orientation, and any other identifier.** A couple of things here: I'm no expert in what's required to put all on equal footing as they grow up and matriculate in our imperfect world (yes, that means outside the USA as well), so I'll leave that to the experts. I'm open to a lot of things. I believe a proactive approach is needed, but note I'll never be a proponent of messaging that seeks to divide us instead of bring us together. We need everyone in the tent to get to where we need to be.

That's it. That's my personal mission statement that guides my view of leadership and managing talent in today's world.

If you've ever felt rudderless or at risk as a manager of people, I'd encourage you to develop your own mission statement for talent in these troubled times we live in.

You don't even have to share it. Simply putting what's most important to you will help you stay grounded in times of uncertainty.

---

2. Reese Bobby's career-day appearance in his son's classroom could be a leadership book on its own, complete with an image of his beverage of choice (Laughing Clown Malt Liquor) on the cover.

4

Becoming a Career Agent Is the Obvious Play

I will not rest until I have you holding a Coke, wearing your own shoe, playing a Sega game featuring you, while singing your own song in a new commercial, starring you, broadcast during the Super Bowl, in a game that you are winning, and I will not sleep until that happens. I'll give you fifteen minutes to call me back.
—Tom Cruise as Jerry Maguire, *Jerry Maguire*

We live in a world that is desperate for exposure and feeling special. Thanks a lot, Mark Zuckerberg!

The need for the masses feeling like stars starts with trophies for all in youth sports, continues with the college admission process,[1] and culminates with average young working professionals curating their social feeds like they're Kim Kardashian.

Andy Warhol was right; everyone is going to get their fifteen minutes. It's just going to be via a social post with 3,165 likes rather than a guest spot on network TV.

Mix this reality of "I'm special" with a tight labor market for the rest of our leadership lives, and the reality is clear. Many of those working for you feel like they should be on the fast track, whether they deserve it or not, and they'll jump to another organization just to feel a little bit famous.

---

1. You have to love a system that prides itself on declining acceptance rates as a means for status. WTF.

You could get completely blown up by this trend as a manager of people, or you could do some complete *Karate Kid/Cobra Kai* stuff and use this reality to your advantage.

I say let's evolve and let the chips fall where they may.[2] Let's talk about repositioning yourself as a Career Agent (think Hollywood) for the people who report to you.

What the Hell Is a Career Agent?
I Thought You'd Never Ask.

The most talented team members of your team don't want a boss or a manager. They want a Career Agent.

A boss/manager of people who is a Career Agent is there to get the job done and get business results, but they'll accomplish something very important along the way. A Career Agent, as a manager of people, approaches every assignment to the team, every task, and all feedback through a simple lens related to the team member/employee in question:

What's in it for you to do what I'm asking you to do?

Think about that for a second. Whether you're assigning work, talking about a project, or giving hard feedback for improvement, a boss who is also a Career Agent isn't simply telling you what to do. They're telling you *why* doing what they are encouraging you to do is good for you.

There's a big difference between normal bosses/managers of people and ones who are actively Career Agents.

That difference? The direct reports of Career Agents think their bosses actually give a s**t about them. I'm not talking about empathy, which can be a cheap word these days. I'm talking about advocacy.

---

2. Second best quote from Tyler Durden in 1999's *Fight Club*. My favorite? "You are not your ****ing khakis."

Advocacy over empathy in a manager means dialogue tracks that sound like this:

> "I care about how you feel, but I'm more interested in pushing you to see the game and absolutely crush it in your career so you can thrive workwise, take care of your family, and feel great about who you are professionally."

Of course, not everyone is ready for Career Agent–type advocacy. Some just want their manager to leave them alone, to let them do the basics, and not think about what's next or where they want to go, etc.

To the average employee, that quote feels exhausting.[3]

To the high performer with ambition, that sounds like the boss they want and need.

A funny thing happens with managers who are Career Agents for those who work for them. Word gets around, and they end up with stronger teams.[4] It turns out that the best path toward retention is to have myopic focus on making people better and be unafraid of them leaving you.

Being a Career Agent Is Rooted in Employee Engagement Theory

For the leadership geeks in the house who are uneasy with my overall vibe and seeming pleasure in talking trash about mainstream leadership advice, I'm happy to report that being a Career Agent is reinforced by modern management theory.

---

3. The same employee might want to hear your thoughts about their potential. They just don't want to do the work.
4. Managers who don't earn this respect love to rationalize the love as "being popular" and other forms of denial.

Need proof? Let's look at the 12 questions that comprise Gallup's Q12 Questions, which form the basis for almost every employee engagement survey known to man.

1. I know what my company expects from me.
2. I have the tools to effectively do my job.[5]
3. I have the opportunity to put my best talents to use every day.
4. **In the past week, I have been recognized for strong work.**
5. **My manager, or someone else at work, cares about me as a human being.**
6. **Someone at work promotes my development.**
7. **My opinion matters.**
8. My company's mission makes me feel like my job matters.[6]
9. My fellow employees commit to doing good work.
10. I've made a best friend at work.
11. **Someone has talked to me about my development in the last six months.**
12. **In the last year, I've had learning opportunities at work.**

It doesn't get more traditional, valid, and conservative than the Q12 from Gallup. I've taken the liberty of bolding the ones with the highest potential for you to impact as a Career Agent as you lead your team.

But wait! Career Agents are different than drones who are working a lame action plan from the last employee engagement survey. To become a Career Agent, you have to be ALL IN where every conversation you have with direct reports is approached from the lens of making them as good as they can possibly be, at the expense of almost everything else.

---

5. This one and all the other nonbolded items don't matter much if an employee's manager is kick-a**.
6. Lots of companies try too hard on this one when mission isn't obvious. You're a bank, not saving the manatees.

Never forget this: *great managers of people have gravity that transcends organizational reputation or company culture.*

Talent flees from bad or average managers in great companies. Talent sticks with great managers at mediocre firms.

Double down on what you can control, my friends. Get some personal gravity and stickiness.

What Do Career Agents Do Better Than Their Peers?

That's kind of what the rest of this book is about.

It's easy to say that Career Agents approach every assignment and all feedback through a simple lens related to the team member/ employee development. It's harder to put it in practice.

If we look at one hundred managers of people in an average company, however, the stars in that peer group (the Career Agents) win via the following things:

- » **They give up control of one-on-ones.** There are a lot of different ways to do check-ins, but Career Agents always let the employee go first.[7] Their agenda matters most and the Career Agent asks them to come prepared with what they want to talk about, which is a subtle yet powerful adjustment. The result of this tweak is more opportunities to coach on roadblocks, politics, and more.
- » **They contrast good versus great on a daily basis.** Opportunities for recognition are everywhere (what up Q12), but Career Agents don't stop at simple recognition. The true players give spot praise and add what an additional tweak might be to make it even better. Delivered in the right way, it becomes a team brainstorm between manager and employee on the way to perceived world domination.

---

7. There's nothing more awkward than letting an introverted employee go first in a one-on-one for the first time. Yikes.

» **They never forget the WIIFM.** Every job has things the incumbent would rather not do. The Career Agent never misses an opportunity to tell their direct report why the task at hand is good for them (the "what's in it for me"), even if it's the equivalent of getting a skid mark off a toilet. Note: conversations about unwanted work generally revolve around creating workflow and systems to do that work less often, which is a classic WIIFM move.

» **They help their team members build portfolios.** Career Agents understand the value of promoting great work by team members to anyone who will listen. But they understand in order to recognize and promote that work, it must first be captured. Career Agents help their people capture great outcomes via documentation, presentations, and more, then use that formatting to tell the world about their star.

We'll dig into many of these areas throughout the rest of the book and throw in how Career Agents are different than average managers in core areas like interviewing, goal setting, exploring strengths, daily coaching, managing change, talking money, performance feedback, and more.

Career Agents aren't different than you. They're just more patient and view the world from a unique lens.

Be Fearless in Looking at the World Outside Your Company as a Career Agent

To truly arrive as a Career Agent, you have to let go, my friends.

Letting go means you have to stop worrying about whether an employee/direct report is going to leave you if you develop them into the star you know they can be.

The best way to lean into this fear is to talk about it openly in conversations. Start with your own positioning of your mission as a

Career Agent, then add on clean messaging that you are unafraid of the prospect taking another offer as their value increases. It sounds a little something like this:

> "I'm not here to just grind on you to get results. I'm here to make you better, so you're going to have fun, make more money over time, and accomplish your career goals *while* we get results for the company.
>
> "I'm willing to do that even if it means you promote yourself by taking a better job with another company because we made you better."

That last statement is a hard one for a lot of talented managers. It's also the statement that, once true and combined with the micro practices in the rest of this book, shows you've arrived at the summit and are self-actualized.

If you love something, set it free. If it leaves, but doesn't require a cease-and-desist order for a nonsolicitation clause, you'll know it loves you back.[8]

You'll Know You Have Arrived When Word Gets Around

Actually, I lied in that last section. Simply saying the words about being fearless of a star leaving you doesn't make you the Best Boss Ever.

But people saying you're their Best Boss Ever for all the reasons we've described so far might, right?

Earlier, I used standard employee-engagement survey methodology featuring Gallup tools to show I don't hate all conventional thinking. If you're into the whole employee engagement thing, by

---

8. If they truly love you, they won't try and raid your team once they leave. If they do, they must be crushed.

all means use the Q12 and the questions I bolded earlier to measure manager traction toward the concepts in this book.

But if you really want to find out who the true Career Agents in your company are, recommend your HR team use this verbatim/open-ended response section of your engagement survey and ask the following gem:

> "Other than the manager you work for, who would you most want to work for in our company and why?"

Shots fired. (Wo)man overboard.

When you ask this question (which I've used multiple times), something consistent happens. For every one hundred to two hundred employees in your company, two managers of people will receive 80 percent of the votes.

Why is that? Since the question frees them from considering their own manager, you'll only need to read the "why" portion of the responses to understand.

Employees talk. They know the managers who invest, protect, and grow their people and do so in an authentic, relationship-building way, and those are the managers who get named the Career Agents.

If you're reading this as a manager of people, you want to be named when this question is asked.[9] If you're a C-level or HR leader with control of an engagement survey, add this open-ended question to the mix.

Asking the employees in the field to name names in this fashion is a great modeling exercise and a great thought-starter for leadership teams.

Managers who are true Career Agents get better performance, retention, and innovation than their peers.

#Facts

---

9. It's always fun to watch a leadership team receive the employee survey packet, ignore the science (numerical ratings), and go to the back of the packet to read the verbatim comments. It's where employees go to talk trash.

Bonus

Moneyball for Leaders: How We Know If You're Great

Managing people is part art and part science.

It's *art* because true influence happens in the margins—it's the impromptu conversation with a direct report in the hallway or the subtle show of support in a meeting that no one else notices.

Add these micro performances up in your life as a manager of people, and the world assigns a *subjective value* to your skill in leading a team.

If you're involved in building enough critically acclaimed careers over time, you might even win the lifetime achievement prize at the corporate versions of the Oscars, otherwise known as the much bally-hooed "Collaborator of the Year" award.[1]

What's that? You didn't win it, but someone who's incredibly average at leading teams did?

That's why *The Big Lebowski* once opined, "Yeah, well, that's just, like, your opinion, man."

Subjective views of who's the best at anything are often BS, but these exist because some things are hard to measure, including the following:

» Style
» Grit
» Overall offensiveness level
» Common sense

---

1. We didn't have a Manager of the Year award, so we had to squeeze you in our existing recognition platform. The engraved crystal diamond is going to look great next to your Workday training manual.

You get my drift, and you might guess where this is going. Some of you are expecting me to say that skill in leading others is hard to measure, and it's best to give up and say that "we know it when we see it."

You would be incorrect.

I'm here to say that if you're truly committed to looking at data over time, objective metrics and measurements (*science!*) exist that can tell you exactly who is the best at managing others via the skills outlined in this book, becoming a Career Agent for those who report to them, and generally kicking much ass.

I've got three metrics I'll use to measure you and your peers over time. Think of me as Billy Beane in *Moneyball,*[2] deploying analytics to uncover the hidden gems among you—the masses leading teams across the globes.

Haters will emerge to challenge these analytics. Pay them no mind. They are the cavemen and cavewomen of the subjective world. Numbers, like open fire, scare them.

Hiring Manager Batting Average

Great teams *just don't happen.* They are driven into being by managers who do the following things:

» Consistently interview candidates well and make great hiring decisions, and
» Keep and grow good talent once it is onboarded.

With those realities in mind, I present the metric of *Hiring Manager Batting Average* (HMBA) which works like this:

---

2. The Brad Pitt version, of course, *with* Jonah Hill as my charming sidekick crunching your stats as a manager.

Hiring Manager Batting Average: Defined as a manager's capability to identify great talent, onboard it, and grow it in a way that creates performance, stability, and retention. To calculate HMBA, use this formula:

<All employees hired by manager over time period still with company after one year>/<All employees hired by manager over time period, including those who have left>

Here's a simple example from a manager I've worked with. Over a three-year period, the manager made eight total hires, and five spent at least a year with the company and as a part of her team. Do the math (five divided by eight) and the HMBA for the manager in this example is .625.[3]

If you like this metric, you know the dirty secret. Hiring Manager Batting Average measures a lot of things beyond simply hiring well, including the following:

1. The manager's ability to provide a realistic job preview and set goals.
2. The manager's ability to successfully onboard talent.
3. The manager's ability to engage and stay connected to talent through all the techniques we'll cover through the rest of this book.
4. The manager's ability to make the employee believe that the job they're in is the best place for them to grow.

That's Hiring Manager Batting Average in a nutshell. It's not just about hiring well, it's about the skills of the manager on Day One and beyond. The one-year mark is a fair threshold, since almost no one leaves a job in the first year unless things are incredibly messed up.

---

3. What's a good HMBA? While it's dependent on the types of jobs you manage, it's fair to say a good HMBA for white-collar professional positions is .850. Target HMBA decreases for hourly positions, but it is still relevant.

It's impossible to hide from this metric over time. If you're sort of toxic or just simply ineffective, some people will walk and find another job in the first year. While one or two of these can happen to anyone occasionally for reasons beyond their control, over time the numbers never lie.

The best managers engage and keep their employees past the one year mark at a higher rate than their peers over time. Period.

Leadership Gravity

If you liked the question I shared in the Career Agent chapter (other than the manager you work for, who would you most want to work for in our company and why?), you're going to love *Leadership Gravity.*

You know what gravity is, right? It's the force an object holds that pulls other objects closer. As it turns out, leadership has gravity inside your organization. Leadership gravity is the extent to which any manager in your organization gets more transfers in than transfers out.

Let's dig in a little bit. Discard all terms that happen when employees leave your company. Only think about internal transfers within your company. Now, run reports on where those transfers went. Tally up the plus/minus for any manager, department, or executive and you've got the relative Leadership Gravity of that person within your company.

If more people want to join you than want to leave you within your company across time, you've got Leadership Gravity.

Leadership Birth Rate

Great leaders and managers are always looking to grow the individual contributor talent they have. They're delegating important tasks to employees, having career conversations with them, and doing a multitude of other things that create engagement and excitement for those who report to them.

As a result, quality leaders give birth to more managers of people per capita than average leaders. You know this to be true, but you've never tried to measure it.

> **Leadership Birth Rate (LBR)** measures the percentage of individual contributor employees from any manager, department, or division who grow up to become managers of people in your company (or beyond your company, if you want to be super progressive).[4]

Your company needs future managers and leaders. You'll need to have a special eye for talent and develop the hell out of the folks who work for you to lead your company in Leadership Birth Rate.

You Probably Won't Be Great at All of These
Stop Worrying about Small Sample Size

In closing, allow me to address some of the things you feel in your gut related to these manager quality metrics/analytics.

You probably won't dominate all three metrics. Your first job as a manager is to make great hires and support them with the tools in this book, which allows you to maximize your batting average. Don't dismiss the metrics because you have a small team, because it all normalizes across time.[5] Misses happen. Stay the course and do better next time.

---

4. You'll know you've arrived on LBR when they start referring to your family tree of leaders who started their careers with you, aka the "Belichick Family Tree."
5. About small teams and whether all this applies: Anyone can go "0 for 1." But if you go "1 for 3" or "2 for 4" on HMBA, it's probably time to acknowledge you have some work to do, right?

For my executives and talent leaders out there, a great way to look at all of these analytics is to roll them up. Look at the roll up of these metrics across functional areas, locations, and business units for great insights. The bigger the headcount in the unit, the harder it is to hide from the realities.

You are what your record says you are.[6]

As you work on becoming a Career Agent for your people as an individual manager, your HMBA goes up, followed by an increase in people internally wanting to join your team (gravity), and former direct reports becoming leaders (LBR).

Me? I'll be over here with my analyst, running formulas, looking at spreadsheets on HMBA and LBR, and admiring the great work you've done.

---

6. Quote from Bill Parcells, who once famously said the following about recruiting: "If they want you to cook the dinner, at least they ought to let you shop for some of the groceries."

5
Leadership Math: The Best Boss Ever Formula

I stopped understanding math when the alphabet decided to get involved.
—Anonymous

So what have we learned so far about this hard-knock life of leadership?

The old ways are too hard, the new ways might be too soft, each of us is prewired with manager-of-people DNA that can stall us out on the corporate ladder, and modern culture demands we focus on the careers of our underlings lest they not feel like the beautiful and unique snowflakes they are.

Add all that stuff up, and it's easy to dream about the glory days when you didn't have a team. It was just you, and you rocked it!

Don't go back; stay in the game. Let's give you a framework that helps you get your head around what's required to thrive as a manager of people and feel guilt free about getting things done through your team. At times, you might even <gasp> delegate and follow up aggressively to get things done through your team without guilt or apology.

I call this framework the *Best Boss Ever Formula*. Whatever cocktail you drink at the bar or at Starbucks, think of it as mixology for your career as a manager.

It's a lifestyle, baby.

The Machine Doesn't Work Unless the Algorithm Is Right: The Best Boss Ever Formula

You've got a set amount of time and interactions with your team. To optimize your tools, drive better dialogue, and maximize performance, the Best Boss Ever Formula appears below:

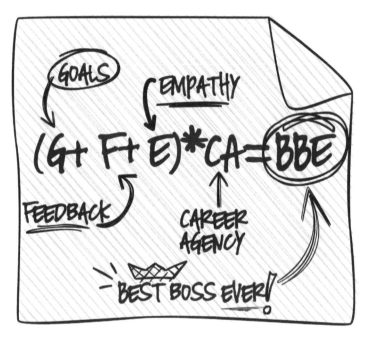

The elements are pretty straightforward, but let's list them out anyway:

- » **Goals** are the targets you set for your team members to get things done and hopefully add incremental value. *This is the equivalent of hope.*
- » **Feedback** is the sum and quality of the observations you make to reinforce the good stuff and redirect on things that could be improved to meet the goals in question. *This is spirit of applause or you kicking someone's rear end, depending on the day.* The trick is to make it sound like a normal conversation whether you're thrilled or pissed.

» **Empathy** is the capacity of comprehending what your direct reports are experiencing from their frame of reference. It means you can place oneself in another's position. Connecting and relating to direct reports is leadership empathy in its purest form. *This is meant to feel like the professional version of—obviously—hugs!* Think side hug, not frontal hug, maybe with a pat on the back and affirmative head nod as you break if you're really feeling it.

» **Career Agency** is a broad term for the perspective and actions that Career Agents take as described in Chapter 4. *This is you as a shameless Hollywood agent, attempting to jump your guy/gal to the front of the line to star in the corporate equivalent of Weekend at Bernie's V.*

To get your head around this, let's assume you spend two hours per week interacting with each member of your team across various mediums—live conversations, Zoom/Teams, email, and passive-aggressive texting.[1] That's 100 hours per year. What percentage of those hours are spent on the various activities above?

It's a hard exercise, right? Left to your own devices and behavioral DNA, you're going to settle into one of the manager-of-people personas we outlined in Chapter 3 (I'm guessing "Control Freak" for you, Skippy). But if we're honest with ourselves, we all have some opportunities to look at this formula and adjust our time allocations.

Find the optimized mix of these strategies in the formula, and you end up becoming a manager of choice—a Best Boss Ever. The relative amounts of goal setting, feedback, and empathy may differ by employee, but once you find the right mix of the first three components of the formula, your outcomes are impacted and multiplied by Career Agency.

---

1. Pro tip: Have a professional writing journal to take notes and track your thoughts as you talk to your people. Your yellow notepad is embarrassing, and no one believes you have any control over where those go once you fill them up.

The more you focus on being a Career Agent, the more you win. Let's dig in a bit to each element of the Best Boss Ever Formula.

Goal Setting Sounds Simple, but Most People Screw It Up

Ah, goal setting. Never has something sounded so simple but been so hard. If you disagree with that statement, you're discounting the complexity and have probably been known to say things like, "I think *The View* does a good job digging into the issues."[2]

Of everything that falls into the BBE formula, managers will likely spend the least time with goal setting, and that's appropriate. The danger isn't in the time allocated, it's in how the tools are used.

Goal-setting traps that can render future conversations on performance DOA include the following:

» **The right goal type depends on the employee.** Low performers need basic goals. High performers need goals that create open-ended conversations. Choose wisely or you'll be sending an honors student to consumer math.

» **Great feedback doesn't happen unless you pick the right goal type.** Goals can create open or closed feedback loops for managers based on which ones you use. Left to their own devices, both organizations and managers alike choose closed loop designs to avoid the messiness of . . . you know . . . actually talking to people.

We'll dig into goal types in a later chapter. For now, just know that we generally suck at goal setting, regardless of tools used. Even (insert heavenly music for effect) cascading goals provided from the top of your organization won't save you from this reality.

---

2. Before you email me about calling out *The View*, just substitute whatever show with some authority you feel is hopelessly lightweight. I'm sure I'll agree.

This Just In: Feedback Is Nuanced As ****

The whole world is a stage, my friends. It's just that most of us are desperately unrehearsed.

We're going to present you with a lot of tools in this book to *give* feedback, as well as one or two to *get* feedback. Once goals are set, feedback is the warning sensor on your Tesla that prevents you from maiming the Grandma whose Ford Taurus has veered into your lane.[3]

Translation: It should always be on, and once in a while it should save your life.

But feedback is incredibly nuanced, as evidenced by these hard truths:

» **It's got to sound like a normal conversation.** You can't fake the tools we're going to give you. Learn them. Know them. Live them. When people don't know you're actually in feedback tool mode, that's when you'll know you've arrived.

» **You have to let your people participate.** Hell, I like the sound of your voice as well. It's *movie-trailer-voiceover* good. But if you do all the talking during feedback convos, your people are going to give you the cosmic equivalent of the middle finger.

» **At times, you'll think you might be spending too long in the feedback loop.** You're wrong. The feedback loop is all about spending twenty minutes when you could have gotten it done in two. In that twenty minutes comes patience, relaxation, and the art of being the Best Boss Ever.

Feedback isn't easy, but once you learn to use the tools we'll provide, wrapped with your own personality, you'll be on your way.

---

3. And yes, just like Tesla's autopilot, occasionally feedback doesn't work and someone gets scarred. You still gotta use it.

Empathy Is the Bridge to Future Performance, Kids

Some of you naturally understand how others feel and ooze it to the outside world.

Others are low on sensitivity, which has the advantage of being quick to recover from brutal feedback, but the Achilles heel is having zero Spidey sense that your direct report is thinking about wiping their hard drive and walking away from society, not to mention your project team.

Becoming someone's Best Boss Ever requires that you have empathy or *develop the appearance of empathy.*[4] Think of being empathetic as an investment of time that allows you to make a withdrawal of performance at a later date.

No deposit, no delivery, Sparky.

If you're empathy challenged (overall or perhaps because you're having a rough week), consider the following strategies to show your direct reports you're feeling their pain:

» **Let them vent and talk it out like you're Dr. Melfi from the Sopranos.** We'll lead with the fact that you have to put in the time. They're going to rant, and you are going to want to interrupt and tell them to suck it up so you can get back to your life. Don't do it. Let it go. Let them vent. Invest.

» **Acknowledge that some s**t is just hard.** Your people probably need to hear from you that you didn't expect it to be easy. Share the wisdom that you expected the struggle, and if you're really feeling the therapy, share a time where you struggled.[5] Too much? Okay, maybe just acknowledge that it's rough out there and shut up again.

» **Brainstorm like there are no bad ideas.** Ah, yes, you're the boss. So after the venting session when your heart rate seems to

---

4. Meaning if you have no empathy, it's your job as a manager to still fake care and spend the time. That's the gig.

5. Don't share your past failures every time someone's struggling. No one wants to work for a loser. #Balance

be returning to 100 bpm, it's time to brainstorm ideas. Danger! Telling them what to do is not coaching. Helping them come up with the solution is the biggest gift you can provide.

» **Refuse the urge to do it for them.** I see you, you complete cyborg. You just want to do it for them, don't you? Go ahead, if you want to live a life of not being able to delegate anything to this person again. Otherwise, stick with the process and spend the time with the ideas above.

Empathy is a process, not a state of mind, for managers of people. If you don't care how others feel, keep being mean on the inside and learn to be the world's greatest listener on the outside.

Yes, She Just Offended the CFO—You Still Have to Be Her Career Agent

Since we've already spent a chapter digging into the profile of a Career Agent, we'll leave you with this tasty morsel from the book of managing others:

> You're going to want to politically disown talented people who embarrass you. These are the people who need a Career Agent the most.

Consider the header of this section. You've got a direct report, who's historically a good performer. There's just one problem. They've offended a C-level employee or otherwise caused a VIP to think of them as a problem. How it happened doesn't matter, and if you're in a highly political organization, there's pressure on you to write them off and agree with the conventional wisdom that they're DOA.

Average leaders abandon and distance themselves from this type of direct report. Real Career Agents realize that the easy stuff is pushing for more when times are good. The hard stuff is helping someone recover from a career-threatening mistake, first via the gift of brutal feedback and second via a plan for reclamation.

If you believe in the direct report, you're there in good times and in bad.

Our formula shows Career Agency as a multiplier force toward becoming a leader of choice. There's nothing that compounds this effect more than you digging in and helping someone when things go sideways for them in your organization.

People watch and people talk.

Be there for people as a Career Agent, even when they might not deserve it.

Do You Have Your Own Gravity as a Leader? A Quiz

DO YOU HAVE YOUR OWN GRAVITY AS A LEADER? A QUIZ.

Audience participation time.
Be brutally honest with yourself to get the most out of this book.

THE QUESTIONS	CIRCLE YOUR ANSWER 1 = Never | 5 = All The Time				
I allow my direct reports to participate in goal setting AND make sure some of their ideas are the ones we use.	1	2	3	4	5
I've talked to my direct reports about what they want to do next (after the job they're in) and refer to it at least once a month in detailed feedback I give them.	1	2	3	4	5
My direct reports know what's merely good versus great in the work they do from my perspective. When I push them to do great work, I always position it from the standpoint of how it can help their career.	1	2	3	4	5
I routinely give my direct reports advice on how to gain leverage and authority in difficult situations at work. I'm unapologetic about helping them succeed, even if it could be perceived as negative by others.	1	2	3	4	5
My direct reports will tell you I want them to succeed, including the fact that I'm on record as being okay if that means they have to leave our organization to advance in their career.	1	2	3	4	5

Total Up Your Points Here:

KD KRIS DUNN

GRADE IT!!

DO YOU HAVE YOUR OWN GRAVITY AS A LEADER? A QUIZ.

When it comes to your skill as a leader and manager of people, **your approach matters.** Managers who are Career Agents retain talent regardless of company-level challenges, and awful managers operating in great cultures have high turnover. Your approach as a leader/manager of people matters more than your company brand.

So how much gravity do you have as a manager of people? First, subtract three points from the total you came up with on the quiz to control for your own "I'm awesome/pretty damn good" bias, then use the scale below to score yourself.

18 TO 25 POINTS

If we're talking about gravity, you're Jupiter. You're actually being listed frequently on "other than your current manager, who would you most like to work for" questions we pitched in the previous chapter. You have many moons.

11 TO 17 POINTS

You're Earth, Venus, or Mars—a midsize planet. You have some believers on your team, but you're still a bit too clinical on this stuff. This book is going to be good for you.

5 TO 10 POINTS

Remind me, is Pluto still a planet? You have limited gravity and are pretty cold in your approach to leading others, aka Mr. or Mrs. Roboto. Let's get you some base tools to use moving forward.

Regardless of your score, we've got some great tools for you. Let's keep moving!

 KRIS DUNN

6

The Lululemon Files: Nine-Boxing for the Win

*I'd never worked in fashion or retail. I just
needed an undergarment that didn't exist.*
—Sarah Blakely, Founder of Spanx

At the intersection of fitness, style, brand, and elitism sits Lululemon.[1]

Lululemon doesn't expect everyone to pay top dollar for something you can buy at Target for one-tenth of the cost. Lululemon knows that based on the brand, there's a group (let's call them the *Naturals*) that will pay whatever it costs to slide into its Instagram-ready stretch pants and other forms of Lulu athleisure.

The more this core group buys, the better Lululemon does. This they know.

But Lululemon is also interested in two other segments: the *Aspirationals* and the *Misfits*. The Aspirationals are the mass market for Lululemon, the group that is thinking about whether the product, price, and utility fit their needs and their own personal brand. The Misfits are the folks who don't think about Lululemon at all and would be a meme-ready mismatch for the brand if they suddenly appeared in your social stream in the company's gear.

To maximize growth, Lululemon wants to find the sweet spot in converting as much of the Aspirational market as possible without eroding the brand cachet and pricing power the company holds.

---

1. I know the company name isn't capitalized because they're trendy AF, but it's the way I'm doing it here.

They also want to avoid Misfit adoption as it runs counter to everything the company's core customer holds to be true.

Flash to the future. If Lululemon is acquired by Apple, you'll know they won big. If you see the company's logo on the overstuffed bargain racks at TJ Maxx and your Uncle Jimmy is rocking the brand, it will be clear that something's gone horribly wrong.

You can learn a lot as a manager of people from Lululemon, and it has nothing to do with your undergarment lines. Let's dig in.[2]

Your Segmentation Starts with a Nine-Box Grid: Performance versus Potential

So here we are. I've presented you with a formula to become your version of the Best Boss Ever, which places a premium on Career Agency, meaning you'll approach almost every conversation from the lens of the employee's career.

Some of you are 100 percent bought in. Other are skeptical at some level. To both parties, I offer this pragmatic, jaded advice:

> You can't become a great manager of people unless you
> adjust the tools for the audience in front of you.

One size fits all rarely works. For best results and to avoid rolling eyeballs and snickering behind your back,[3] you'll need to adjust your delivery on an employee-by-employee basis.

Enter the *Performance versus Potential nine-box grid* (which I'll call PvP from here on out).

The PvP is one of the most widely used tools in succession planning and development.

It assesses your people in two simple dimensions:

---

2. Pun 100 percent intended. This might make me a Misfit.
3. Rolling out the same approach for all is from the playbook of the Trend-Spotter/Reader of Bestsellers, who love to flex leadership tools to all in the same way with zero customization. Cringe. It's hard to see people mocked.

» Their past performance.

» Their future potential.

I'll let you go research this to your heart's content elsewhere. For now, just know the obvious; your best employees exist around the top-right corner of the PvP, and the employees who struggle cluster to the bottom left.

All the others? Yeah, that's kind of what the *manager of people* tag is all about, my friends.

Let's Slice and Dice Your Market as a Manager of People Like Lululemon

Flash back to Lululemon trying to sell $150 pants. If they were to create a nine-box grid to segment their potential customers, they might use "fit for our brand" and "willingness to pay" on the x- and y-axes. Add the aforementioned persona names (Naturals, Aspirationals, and Misfits), and you end up with segmentation that looks something like this:

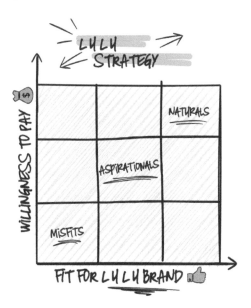

But wait! I've taken the liberty of showing Performance and Potential on the x- and y-axes as well to show you that thinking about types of employees and personas is a must in your day-to-day life as a manager of people.

Approach the advice in this book with a same-size-fits-all approach and you'll be called a Tony Robbins clone by many. I like Tony Robbins![4] But motivation prose doesn't—wait for it—motivate everyone. That's why it's up to you to adjust your approach for the person in front of you.

Different Strokes for Different Folks: Know Your Audience

The tags and segmentation I used for Lululemon can easily apply to your day-to-day life as a manager of people. Your day moves fast, and every hour finds you talking to someone different in front of you.

Naturals, Aspirationals/Climbers, and Misfits are all looking for something different from you and respond to different things. The tools are the same, but the application differs depending on who you're talking to.

Cliff notes:

» **The Naturals:** As the highest performers on your team, Naturals want to be treated differently. They have career options, tons of ambition, and, this just in—some in this group consider themselves more talented than you and might even want your job. It's easy to be defensive or guarded with a Natural when you feel the ambition burning you like you forgot to put on the SPF 50.

But rolling out the ole "I'm fair and treat everyone the same" lameness is a path to multiple forms of pain with this group. The Natural will seek career guidance elsewhere if you're not going

---

4. For the cleanest dive into Tony Robbins, watch *I Am Not Your Guru* on Netflix. It's like watching a car crash.

to provide it, and you'll be seen as an average manager in your organization as a result. They'll also be quicker to leave the organization as a result of a "treating everyone equally" approach.

The answer for managing Naturals is simple. Use the BBE formula with heavy doses of Career Agency for best results. "I think you're great, let's figure out how to get you where you want to be" is the path in all conversations with the Natural that we'll cover as we move forward. Think of yourself as *Karate Kid's* Mr. Miyagi—humble, at times underestimated, but the master of mind tricks designed to move the student forward.[5] Wax on, wax off, you crafty seeker of knowledge.

» **The Aspirationals:** Steady performers and good citizens for the most part, Aspirationals want what they consider to be their just due—credit for a job done well. Was their performance on the job in question good or great? That's kind of the question at hand whenever you're dealing with the Aspirationals. They've long been told that they're the glue that's holding the leaky ship you call a company together, but they haven't gotten a lot of critical feedback as a general rule.

Some Aspirationals have ambition and want more, but some don't. As a result, your best path forward with this group is to provide recognition for steady performance that "meets" expectations as a reward. Once that's completed, proceed with caution and describe what could be added to the performance in question to make it great, not merely good.

If the additional feedback sparks a healthy back-and-forth conversation, you've got a live one, Jenny! Regardless of the reaction, all Aspirationals enjoy conversations that focus on their career development. Why? Because 90 percent of your employees think they're in the top 10 percent of performers.[6] This group likes to be talked to like an emerging star even though some of

---

5. Fifty-seven percent of the answers you need as a manager of people are included in *Karate Kid*. More Miyagi on a daily basis, people.
6. Among my most jaded lines in this book, but hey, you know it's true.

them will never follow through with the discretionary effort it takes to advance.[7]

» **The Misfits:** I know what you're thinking. All this Career Agent talk doesn't work with low performers. You're right and wrong at the same time. Talking to someone about where they want to go in their career and the Maserati-like performance it's going to take to get there doesn't make sense for the Misfit. But wait—being a Career Agent for the Misfit works with slight modifications.

Start with what Misfits need. They need to stay employed with your company. That means every tool we'll discuss in the rest of the book—coaching, performance management, and more—can and should be used to migrate someone from being at risk of being fired to being safe and performing in a way that doesn't make you need blood pressure medication.

Career Agency for the Naturals is about setting them up for what's next, getting out of the way, and being available. The Aspirationals require an approach that focuses on the contrast of good versus great. Misfits require you to migrate them from being at risk to being merely good.

Lululemon isn't interested in migrating all Aspirationals and Misfits into their customer base. For you, as a manager of people, it's a must.

---

7. I feel like 33 percent of the Aspirationals have the intestinal fortitude, drive, and ambition for the climb you're offering. The rest just like hearing it, and that's okay—the world needs ditch-diggers, too.

Part II

Core Stuff to Master

7

You're Job Is to Predict the Future in Less than 60 Minutes

(Interviewing & Selection)

*A job interview is not a test of your knowledge
but your ability to use it at the right time*
—Unknown

Know Thyself and Have a Freaking Plan

When it comes to interviewing, it pays to know thyself and have a plan to save yourself.

If you don't have an agenda, you're going to BS at will, have a great time with the perfectly likeable candidate in front of you, and of course, simply make a gut call on the candidate without learning anything in your time together. Ugh. Winner: the Candidate.[1] Loser: you (especially when you have to term them five months later or they leave voluntarily).

---

1. The long tail of unconscious bias. Not interviewing well means you hire more people like yourself. Gross.

Tool 1: Sample Timeline for a One-Hour Interview
The Perfect Interview Plan That Blends
Getting Info and Selling

Whatever you like to do most, the following interview plan still emphasizes your strengths. You can dig into the résumé in the KSA (knowledge, skills, and abilities) section and show how likeable you are (important) in the opening and closing section. We've budgeted some time to BS and give the candidate what they expect via the intros/small talk section, the Five-Minute Résumé Review ("walk me through the résumé and then we'll dig in") and the Q&A section at the end.[2]

The Perfect Interview Plan

Step	Time (minutes)
Introductions	10
Questions about applicant	30
Position-specific discussions	15
Conclusion	5
Total	60

The simple stuff works best. Save yourself from many of the aforementioned reasons we suck at hiring by having a plan, and stick to the time allocations. You'll get the best information possible if you touch all the lines.

---

2. The real pros will make the whole interview seem like a conversation, but it's not. They're sneaky like that.

Tool 2: The Behavioral Interviewing STAR
*Get Out of the Business of Asking for Hypotheticals
and Use Behavioral Interviewing*

I normally run full-day sessions on interviewing and selection, so I'm going to focus on the most important things here to help you suck less at interviewing.

Without a plan or formal training, many reading this book wouldn't wade into the wizardry of *Behavioral Interviewing*. That's a shame because it's not that hard.

To get started with behavioral interviewing, think about the strengths you need beyond the résumé. These are called behavioral dimensions and include things you want to know about the candidate, such as initiative, dealing with adversity, handling difficult people, working for an awesome boss (to get them ready for working for you, ha), etc. Once you have the dimensions you want to explore, line up behavioral interview questions that help you explore the area with a candidate.[3]

Behavioral interview questions begin by asking for specifics, not hypotheticals. Questions typically start out, "Tell me about a time" or "Describe a situation," which are designed to move candidates away from generalities and to specific circumstances and things they dealt with from their past.

Smooth talkers love hypothetical questions. You'll love their hypothetical answers, but they mean nothing—they're the cotton candy of the interviewing process.

Once you ask the behavioral question, you take notes as the interviewer and make sure you have the following elements in the candidate's answer, which is commonly noted as the "STAR."

---

3. I'm linking a list of possible dimensions and 300 plus potential behavioral questions in the web resources. You're welcome.

S	SITUATION	DETAIL THE BACKGROUND. PROVIDE A CONTEXT WHERE? WHEN?
T	TASK	DESCRIBE THE CHALLENGE AND EXPECTATIONS WHAT NEEDED TO BE DONE? WHY?
A	ACTION	ELABORATE YOUR SPECIAL ACTION. WHAT DID YOU DO? HOW? WHAT TOOLS DID YOU USE?
R	RESULTS	EXPLAIN THE RESULTS: ACCOMPLISHMENTS, RECOGNITION, SAVINGS, ETC. QUANTIFY

STAR TECHNIQUE TO LISTEN TO BEHAVIORAL INTERVIEW ANSWERS

Simple right? Just take notes as the candidate talks across these three areas and figure out what you don't have and follow up accordingly. But wait . . .

Tool 3: How to Spot Fake Answers to Interview Questions
Please Activate Your Fiction Detector

The candidate in front of you is going to spit out stuff that sounds great but isn't meaningful for you to use to figure out what they can actually do as a part of your team.

Don't hold it against them, the world encourages them to do it.

False STARs are answers to behavioral questions that are glittering generalities. They're responses that are either opinions, theoretical, vague, or future-oriented. They don't actually tell you what a candidate did in the past. They sound great but aren't real answers to the behavioral questions you're going to ask.

How can you identify BS answers that don't help you?

You know within the first 10 seconds of an answer that you're getting junk if the scenario they are describing sounds like these examples:

» **Theoretical or future-oriented.** Tells you what a candidate "would" do in the future ("What I usually do in that situation is . . .").
» **Vague statements.** Sound good but contain no specifics on what a candidate actually did ("My team at Microsoft had that situation, we handled it by . . .").
» **Opinions.** Tells you how a candidate feels or thinks but not what they actually did ("I believe that the key in dealing with idiots is . . .").

The key in combating BS answers is identifying them early in the candidate's response (is the situation or task real from the candidate's past? Is the action they are giving you actually what *they* did in the past?) and redirecting the candidate.

Saying word tracks like this helps to redirect the candidate and get what you need:

> "Let me jump in here, what I'm actually looking for is a specific situation that comes to mind from your past, and what you did specifically to deal with that situation."

> "Tell me about the last time you used that approach."

Your mom told you not to interrupt people. She was right, except when it comes to hearing a bad answer in an interview. You have to get in and redirect, or you're going to listen to three to five minutes of stuff you can't use.[4]

---

4. Pro tip: Start this part of the interview by telling them what you're looking for and that you're likely to jump in and redirect at times. Explain why it's in their best interest that you do that. Prepare them to be interrupted and it's cool.

These redirects help you ask for a micro, specific situation that was challenging and allow you to follow up for more detail in a smart way.

As soon as you hear phrases like the ones shown here that tell you you're dealing with some BS, interrupt as quickly (and professionally) as you can.

Tool 4: How to Follow Up to Dig in More after the Initial Answer
Follow Up Like You're Interrogating the Unabomber

As you define a *time* or a *situation* that's real and not hypothetical BS, you'll need to probe further for more depth or detail with questions like these:

» "What were you thinking at that point?"
» "Tell me more about your meeting with that person."
» "Lead me through the decision-making process that led you to that plan."

Note that almost all of these follow-ups happen in the "Action" portion of the STAR. You want to know everything about *what they did* in the situation at hand. If you're being told a story that's anything but totally honest, the response will generally not hold up through the barrage of probing questions.

Remember, you're using the behavioral interview technique to evaluate a candidate's experiences and behaviors so you can determine potential for success as part of your team. Eighty percent of the total time of your interview should be spent understanding what they did ("Action" in the STAR format) and why, given the situation the candidate laid out for you.

Be curious and ask a bunch of follow-up questions.[5] If you simply listen, take notes, and don't ask for more, you lose in a big way. Follow-up questions about the job, their last boss, process, tools, the company, and more are all fair game—the more specifics you get, the more you win.

Time of Possession Matters—So Don't Forget to Shut Up

If you're talking (as the hiring manager) in the interview 50 percent of the time or more, you're losing in a big way, my friend. Your goal should be to be personable, set the stage, make the candidate comfortable, and get them talking.[6]

Shoot for a 20:80 time of possession target (where you talk 20 percent of the time and the candidate talks 80 percent). When you have to redirect the candidate or follow up, get in and out quickly. Remember, if your original question or follow-up questions last more than 15 seconds, the candidate will forget what the ****ing question actually was.[7]

You think I'm joking. I can assure you I'm not!

Remember that people like me (recruiters) routinely tell candidates that if the interviewer does all the talking, the candidate should let them. That narcissist hiring manager is going to leave the session and think it went great because they—wait for it—did all the talking.

Shut up and don't dominate time of possession in the interview to win.

---

5. I'll always take the curious interviewer. The more you follow up, the more you get the morsel that matters.
6. Yes, I'm looking at you, extroverts. You're going to want it to be a 50/50 conversation or more. Don't do it.
7. Big danger in putting prepared questions in your own words; you become a rambling, imprecise doofus.

Don't Forget to Sell and Be the Best Host(ess) Since Oprah

The biggest error you can make as a hiring manager in today's hiring environment is to assume the burden is only on the candidate.

All things being relatively equal across different job opportunities, the candidate you most want to add to your team will make the decision based on *who they want to work for and who they most connected with.*

With that in mind, you should treat all candidates like a VIP on interview day, make efforts to connect, and be genuinely interested in all of them. Don't be a freaking robot.

You never know which candidate is going to be The One.[8] They all have choices, so act accordingly.

---

8. Make everyone want to work for you and be appropriately crushed if they don't get the job. That's show business.

KD'S CHEAT SHEET:
INTERVIEWING CANDIDATES

DO THIS!

- Have an interview plan and stick to it.
- Make it all sound like a normal conversation while you ruthlessly get all the information you need and more.
- Use Behavioral Interviewing to ask for specifics.
- Listen closely and don't accept hypothetical answers.
- Be awesome.
- Use at least three to five follow up questions to understand more about candidate experience and capabilities.
- Sell, baby, sell!

WATCH OUT FOR THESE TRAPS!

- Don't start small talk and suddenly realize you're 20 minutes into an hour interview and have accomplished nothing.
- Don't be mesmerized by a smooth-talking candidate who talks in glittering generalities and sounds like a politician.
- Are you sitting behind your desk like it's 1982?
- Don't simply accept a candidate's seemingly credible answer without following up for more.

RESOURCES FOR YOU ONLINE - BESTBOSSEVER.ORG

- Comprehensive list of behavioral interview questions by dimension
- STAR Note-Taking Guide for Interviews
- "If this, then that" follow-up questions when you hear soft, nonspecific answers to your questions

MORE FUN STUFF ONLINE

- Interview scene clips from *The Internship* and *Transformers 3*

 KRIS DUNN

Bonus

I've Got Ten Minutes, Impress Me

(The Art of Exploring Motivational Fit)

Can the candidate in front of you do the job? Sure.

Will they want to do it for a long period of time at your company? That depends. After all, it's total chaos in that freak show you call a company.

That, my friends, is why I'm following up the deep primer on interviewing with the simpler topic of *Motivational Fit*.

There are two types of brutal misses when it comes to hiring: you completely whiffing on a hire,[1] or you making a good hire on paper but failing to figure out if the candidate likes to work or is a fit for your circus.

Motivational Fit questions are the technical equivalent of you saying to the candidate:

> "Don't try and fake me out, are you actually going to want to do the job I have for you?"

You'll see a lot of candidates who can do the job in question. What you need to be sure of is that they'll want to do that job, *at your company, working for you*, over an extended period of time. Think about the role in question, then expand that role to all the possible tasks/projects. Now, add in the craziness of how your team

---

1. This is when you miss and you look back and say, "What was I smoking that day?"

works, your management style, and the company's overall function or dysfunction.

The result of those combinations is that it can be anyone's guess whether even a qualified candidate can actually be happy working for your combination of *job/manager/team/company*. That's why you have to dig deeper and consider motivational fit.

Let's start with a simple definition of motivational fit:

> **Motivational Fit:** The "will do" (as opposed to the "can do") evaluation you use to determine whether there is a sufficient match between how a person likes to work and what is available in the job/organization you're a part of to keep them satisfied (motivated).

There are three primary vibes you'll hear from the candidate when you ask questions in the Motivational Fit cluster:

» **Job Fit:** The extent to which activities in the job are consistent with what results in personal satisfaction to a candidate, or the degree to which the work itself will be personally satisfying. Loaded question/consideration![2]

» **Manager/Organizational Fit:** The extent to which a manager/organization's mode of operation and values are consistent with the type of environment that provides personal satisfaction. This is mostly whether the candidate is going to like working with and for you. Dicey at best![3]

» **Team Fit:** The extent to which the composition and work style of the team the candidate will be joining will be satisfying. Will

---

2. "I've often dreamed of working at a company like yours, with rickety systems and lack of true processes."
3. "I love working for flawed people. I've been told it's one of my strengths."

it be perfect harmony or hornet's nest on your team? The truth usually lies somewhere in the middle.[4]

The fact that hypothetical questions are easy to fake (No strengths? Just make some up and sell it baby!) gave rise to the behavioral interview, which attempts to cut through the hype/spin by asking candidates about specific experiences they have had.

Unfortunately, the behavioral interview is only as good as the interviewer. You can ask a behavioral question ("Tell me about a time you had to tell your boss they were wrong"), but if the interviewee gives you hypothetical soft stuff back, you've got to have the ability to interrogate/grind on them about what they actually did when faced with that situation.

That's why I'm adding these Motivational Fit questions to the mix for you. I recommend you always ask questions related to motivational fit as a backup to behavioral interview questions.

It matters so much that, if you only find yourself with ten to fifteen minutes with a candidate, you could skip the behavioral interview questions and go straight to motivational fit (these time limitations can happen if you're doing brief interview conversations in support of one of your hiring peers, or if you are doing a skip-level interview for a manager on your team who is hiring).

To dig in on motivational fit, ask the candidate the following two questions/items designed to evaluate motivational fit and spend five minutes digging into each:

» Tell me when you have been *most satisfied* in your career . . .
» Tell me when you have been *least satisfied* in your career . . .

Those two questions measure Motivational Fit and are stunning in their simplicity. Assuming you like the background and

---

4. "I think teams that resemble *The Purge* create tension where people can do their best work."

experiences of the candidate and are confident they can do the job, you really only need to evaluate if your company, the specific opportunity, and the candidate are a fit for each other.

Once you get the response from the candidate, ask "why is/was that?" and say "tell me more" multiple times.[5] Then stop talking. Shut up. Zip it.

Don't bail the candidate out, but rather force them to tell you what really jazzes them about jobs and companies and, subsequently with the second question, what drives them crazy.

Once you get that, you'll have what you need, and it's analysis time. Candidate likes tons of structure, but all you can provide is the three-ring circus you call a department and/or company? Move on. Candidate likes to play ping-pong for four hours a day, but your CEO walks around evaluating if people are working hard enough by how unhappy they look? Probably not going to work out.

If the candidate truly struggles with the "most satisfied, all-time, across all jobs" approach, you can break down Motivational Fit at their current or past job you're interested in by asking the following questions:

» Tell me about two things in this job (current or past role) that really motivate(d) you.
» Tell me about two things in this job (current or past role) that you hate(d).

Give it a try and spend at least five minutes on each item: most satisfying/least satisfying. Probe not only for job likes/dislikes but also love/hate aspects of their current and past bosses, team, and companies they've been a part of.[6]

You'll be shocked at the value of what candidates tell you in response to these simple questions.

---

5. If the candidate struggles to answer, try, "There's got to be something. What did you like best (or least)? You can pick anything." Once you get a small morsel, you're off to the races.
6. Following up an initial response to these questions with, "I hate that too!" has been known to unleash a waterfall of information you never would have gotten otherwise: Making the Candidate Comfortable 101.

8

Sure, You've Had Four Jobs in the Last Year, but Let's Focus on Your Strengths

(Onboarding New Employees)

It's a very subtle thing to talk about strengths and weaknesses because almost always they're the same thing. A strength in one situation is a weakness in another.
—Steve Jobs

Most of today's leadership thought trendsetters will tell you it's all about strengths, with the clear path to self-actualization and your team loving you existing in a singular focus on what your direct reports do well.

Meanwhile, Allison (your second-year direct report) just destroyed all your momentum via her incredible inability to read the vibe of the room in a throwaway cross-departmental meeting. You've got three emails and a "drop-in" from a colleague of your boss to prove it.[1]

---

1. Real talk. Most leadership books don't capture the range of humanity you face as a manager of people. Allison and the rest of your team are going to cause you and themselves pain on at least a monthly basis. It's part of the job.

Keep playing those "strengths only" YouTube videos and feeling the warm glow, my friends!

Reality check: your job as a Career Agent/Coach for your people should include at least some focus on their career not getting savagely derailed because they hate details, have flatlined empathy, or <insert weakness here>.

There's a way to talk about derailers without being an jerk. It's called *balance*. Let's dig in.

Tool 5: Sample Assessment—Cognitive and Behavioral Dimensions
Stay Away from Your Opinion and Get an Assessment You Can Use

When you initially onboard a new employee, you think you know them. Turns out, you don't know anything.

The first thing to acknowledge when it comes to using strengths and weaknesses is that you need an independent, validated tool to dig into what makes somebody tick. For most of us, this means you need to find a *behavioral assessment* you like and are willing to use as part of your platform.

Many of your HR leaders will provide one for you at your company. In case your company doesn't provide one, here's what to look for when seeking an assessment to understand what your direct reports bring to the table:

» **Find an assessment that has cognitive as well as behavioral measurements.** General cognitive ability is not IQ per se. It's learning ability, the ability to process large amounts of information on the fly, pulling together disparate bits of information, and making quick, accurate decisions. It's an important area to have data on your direct reports. If someone's natural state is to take a week to really dig in, you probably need to know that.[2]

» **Don't overthink what you need with the behavioral side of any assessment you're considering.** It's easy to overengineer your needs. All assessment platforms are going to have similar components such as assertiveness, detail orientation, rules orientation, introversion/extroversion, etc. The deeper you go down the rabbit hole of complexity, the less usable the tool becomes.

» **Your primary report of the assessment you use should be one page in length and visual in nature.** That's right: a single page. There can be additional supporting documentation, but experience shows that's just going to make your eyes glaze over and make you want to grab a nap. What's simple gets used, so control the mad scientist in you and keep it basic.

The dirty little secret to most assessments? They're all based on the same couple of validity studies (Five Factor Model, etc.), which means that having more pages is a user interface and marketing decision, not a statement on precision or value.

There are a lot of good assessment tools out there. Here's an example of the output of the one I use, which I'll refer to as an example the rest of the way.

---

2. When's the last time you heard someone say, "You know what, we need some people who will really take their time to evaluate things around here?" Put your hands down, compliance department.

Assessment of Allison

Damn, Allison! No wonder you blew up that meeting by saying crap you shouldn't have!

Someone should have included some awareness on potential "opportunities" (what the politically correct people call "things that can kill your career") as part of the onboarding of the manager/employee relationship. That sucks for Allison.

Tool 6: How to Map and Discuss Strengths and Weaknesses
*Set an Early Baseline by Mapping Two Incredible
Strengths and Two Potential Weaknesses*

The key to any conversation about strengths and weaknesses is balance. Bottom line, if you're a Career Agent for your people, you get the grace to talk about weaknesses by first talking about strengths early in your manager/employee relationship and by making your people believe over time that you're singularly focused on helping them win.

At the start of any relationship, a great way to establish this yin-yang feedback loop is to take your direct report's assessment profile and *identify two primary strengths and two potential weaknesses.*

Raise Awareness by Identifying Where It Might All Go to Hell
Let's use Allison as an example.

Look back to the previous assessment profile of Allison. If I was running her onboarding onto my team and had access to her assessment at the start of my relationship, a sample "two strengths/two weaknesses" play would have gone something like this:

> **Strengths:** (1) High Cognitive, which means you'll learn quickly and make decisions with speed, and (2) Low Rules, which means you'll deal with the chaos that exists in our high change environment really well. Sweet!

> **Weaknesses:** (1) Highest Assertiveness, which can be a strength but at your level may mean that you bulldoze others if you don't have a lot of self-awareness, and (2) Low Sensitivity, which means you don't always understand how others around you feel. Danger!

No wonder Allison couldn't read the vibe of the room in that throwaway cross-departmental meeting you decided not to attend.[3]

Establishing something as simple as two assessment-based strengths and weaknesses sets you up to be an effective coach and Career Agent.

Absent the assessment, this breakdown is your opinion. With the tool in place, *it's science*.

Go get a tool and set the stage.

Tool 7: How to Create Openness by Sharing Your Own Assessment Profile
Show You're Not a Dictator by Sharing Your Profile

The old ways don't work today. Command and control worked for Don Draper in *Mad Men*, but to be an effective manager in today's world, you're going to have to display something most of us aren't comfortable with.

It's called *vulnerability*.

Calm down. I'm not talking about the type of vulnerability where you tell your team you hid in the closet last night for some "you" time after someone was mean to you.[4] I'm talking about the fact that in order to get your team's attention on weaknesses, you should share your own assessment profile with them. That process goes something like this:

1. Share your assessment profile. I generally recommend doing this after you've covered theirs from a power/authority perspective. The order matters, so sharing your profile is background and context once you've dug into their profile.

---

3. High Cog means people like Allison think they know the answer in 10 seconds (they usually do). Highest Assertiveness means they can't help themselves to shortcut a meeting by telling everyone what the answer is. Ugh.

4. At 9:00 p.m. See the bonus chapter exploring the wisdom of late-night emails. Lots of snowflakes out there.

2. Tell them what you think your strengths and weaknesses are. No, you don't have to let them pontificate and guess. Stay in control and tell them your view, then keep moving, Johnny.

3. Tell them how awareness of potential situational weaknesses has helped you in your career. Story time! Use real-life examples to show them the value of awareness, minus the story about you weeping at work in a bathroom stall.

4. Use the transparency to your assessment profile to talk about the best way to deal with you as a manager. It's an owner's manual for you as their boss when you really think about it. You're full of features, but there's a way to use you as a resource that gets the best results. We'll talk about this in the chapter on manager assimilation sessions, but you should provide direction one-on-one in this area as well.

Bottom line, you have to give in order to get. Share your profile, control the narrative, and you'll open up your people to coaching them on weaknesses as a part of your platform.[5]

Do this in a transparent and authentic way, and you'll find that referring to your own behavioral DNA becomes a seamless, supportive talking point in your coaching conversations directed at your people.

Damn, look at you. All introspective and grown up—in a totally controlled way with limited downside.

Push the Talent to Where They Are Best, but Ask Them to Help Create the Time

All this talk about weaknesses shouldn't hide an obvious fact: strengths do matter! You didn't hire them for the opportunity to provide nonstop therapy.

---

5. Think of this as opening the book on you, giving them a glimpse, and then returning the conversation to them.

A big part of your job is to make sure your people get an opportunity to do what they do best. Remember that one of the key Gallup rating items for employee engagement we cited earlier is *"At work, I have the ability to do what I do best every day."*

What's getting in the way of you doing this as a leader? Simple! Its all the busy work and non-value-add BS that has to get done in any job. It's there for your job as well as the roles each of your direct reports are in.

That is why I'm a big fan of saying something like the following to your people:

> "Let's work together to squeeze down all transactional work, administrivia, and things you don't like to do to the smallest amount of time possible, giving you more time to do stuff that matters."

Do I believe this is valuable? Yes, I do.

Is it a bit of a trap? Why yes! Yes, it is.

Allocating more time to strengths isn't just about mimicking the motivated dude in the TEDx video.

It's easy to say we're going to focus on your strengths, but then the world gets in the way. Reports, busy work, meetings, and more all collude to make it harder than it looks.

A big requirement of being able to use more time on strengths is to handle the noninteresting work in a more efficient manner. And to make that happen, your direct reports have to become more efficient at the things they don't enjoy as much.

So, make the statement and tell them they're part of helping you create the time for the enhanced focus on the good stuff. Don't create additional goals for them until they help you carve down time on the boring stuff.

They have to give in order to get. Some will, some won't.

Tool 8: Weaving Strengths and Weaknesses into Daily Coaching
Coach with the Profile in Mind

Do the right things at the start of your relationship related to strengths and weaknesses, and coaching flows like water.

Goal setting, performance feedback, and daily coaching become easier. It's less about what happened and more about optimization. Behavioral strengths and weaknesses become the context for deeper conversations.

> "I'm putting you on this because you're awesome at _____."

> "When you go into that meeting, be aware of _____ and how you'll naturally react to it."[6]

Deeper knowledge of what makes someone tick and the right initial conversation/set up gives you the inside lane to influence, trust, and higher performance.

In a sea of onboarding noise, it's actually the most important thing you can do in the first month with a new employee. If you're reading this with an established team, refresh your coaching platform by working through this strengths/weaknesses process.

Advantage: You.

---

6. Smart managers do hat tips like the ones listed here in at least a 3:1 ratio over time. Mix three strengths references in for every "make sure you don't kill yourself" tidbit for best results.

KD'S CHEAT SHEET:
ONBOARDING NEW EMPLOYEES

DO THIS!

- ○ Find a behavioral assessment you can use, and put yourself and your team through it.
- ○ Run a session with each direct report to cover two strengths and two weaknesses; discuss the impact of each on the job in question and inside your organization.
- ○ Share your own profile, covering your strengths and weaknesses, and share stories or what you've learned about yourself as a result.
- ○ Laugh out loud at all the times you've screwed up when your noted weaknesses got the best of you.
- ○ Use the identified strengths and weaknesses for your direct reports by weaving them into your routine coaching.

WATCH OUT FOR THESE TRAPS!

- ○ Don't think that it's all going to go well when you're onboarding a new direct report.
- ○ Don't believe the hype that you should only manage via strengths.
- ○ Don't be afraid to talk openly and honestly about how weaknesses can cause career harm in specific circumstances.
- ○ Don't act like you're the bomb and you don't have glaring weaknesses of your own.

RESOURCES FOR YOU ONLINE - BESTBOSSEVER.ORG

- ○ Example behavioral assessment with descriptions (helps you seek your own if you need to)
- ○ Exercise in identifying two strengths and two weaknesses in a direct report (with answers and discussion) to help you get in a groove before you do it with your people
- ○ Talking tracks to help you weave behavioral strengths and weaknesses into daily coaching and overall performance management activities

MORE FUN STUFF ONLINE

- ○ Video clips including Vin Diesel (a great manager of people) discussing team strengths in *Fast & Furious*

 KRIS DUNN

Bonus

And the World Shall Be Led by the One Who Can Execute in Chaos

Spending our first two chapters on selecting the right candidate and onboarding them onto your team is *expected*. You probably yawned a bit when you saw me lead with a chapter on interviewing.

Damn. Tough crowd.

Let's mainline some truth that some will view as op/ed but is as predictable and reliable as Ryan Reynolds playing the exact same quippy character in every movie he stars in.[1]

Most of you are going to suck at hiring early in your careers. As a result of these struggles, the candidate DNA test for grown up, veteran hiring managers is the cognitive and behavioral assessment (the definition of which we covered at length in the last chapter).

Clear preferences have emerged across hiring managers who have battle scars from missing on new hires and use these tools so they won't be fooled again by smooth talkers in interviews.

What have these veterans learned about using these tools, and where do they still make mistakes?

Lucky for you, I've done an anthropology-like tour supporting hiring managers that rivals Margaret Mead in her Oceania studies.

---

1. You know it's true. From *Deadpool* to *Red Notice*, Ryan's the same guy. Smarta** but cute one liners in times of pressure repeated forty-nine times per movie with excellence. Shake your moneymaker, Ryan.

When the primates known as "hiring managers" use assessments, the following are their customs, practices, and blind spots.[2]

Even Veteran Managers Habitually Overreact to a Single Assessment Category

The following conversation is repeated 1,716 times a day in corporate life:

> Me (the talent leader/HR pro/recruiting leader): "I'm going to give you an awesome tool, but you have to be reasonable."
>
> Them (the hiring manager or executive): "Sure, why wouldn't I?"
>
> Me: <Gives them assessment on a candidate they've interviewed and think they might hire.>
>
> Them: "Holy s**t, I can't hire this person!"

And that, my friends, is the first problem with the use of assessments in the hiring process. For all the goodness, many of you won't take a step back and look at the candidate in totality. Instead, you'll see a single category that doesn't look perfect to you or is otherwise wonky and freak the **** out.

This is the equivalent of finding a face freckle on a supermodel (any gender! Don't email me!) and saying, "It was good except for the facial blemish; it's gonna be a no for me dawg."[3]

The refined manager understands the game behind the game. A single area of concern (think dimensions in an assessment) isn't a reason not to hire; it's a coaching note for onboarding. Two areas of

---

2. What follows is best read thinking of me with a tobacco pipe, sitting in a Barcalounger on PBS discussing the strange ways of the creatures I've observed in my time in the field, making the qualitative seem quantitative. LOL.
3. Presented without gender role stereotypes but in pure Randy Jackson/ *American Idol* vibe.

concern (out of ten) means you probably still hire them if you love them in every way.

Three or more areas of concern? At that point, you're right to pass in most circumstances. Go ahead and toss it over to the recruiter most resembling Simon Cowell for the "we've decided to go a different direction" feedback loop.

Smart Managers Always Look at Company Vibe and Culture as Well as the Job

Of course, the same assessment can tell you a lot about how a candidate might fare inside the culture at your company or within your team.[4]

While declining a candidate for a single area of assessment concern related to the job is generally a stretch, mismatches in single areas related to your culture can and should cause rightful concerns.

This is especially true if a candidate exists at the *far extreme in a single area* (often viewed as a super-strength, by the way), and it looks like a mismatch for how your company/team operates in their natural state. Here are a few fun, but real, examples:

» **The Rebel.** This candidate has the lowest rules orientation score known to man (hates structure) and loves chaos, but your company has more processes and procedures than the IRS. Seems like a match! Let's get you two married!

» **The Bully.** Your organization runs on consensus and teamwork. This candidate has the highest assertiveness score possible and interrupted/domineered you in the interview. I liked the guy too!

» **The Diva.** Your team is known as a school of sharks, just swimming around and killing/eating daily with little emotion. The

---

4. Alternatives for the word "culture" include bubble, club, cult, freak show, and circus.

Diva is highest sensitivity and high extroversion, which means you'll need to be a therapist weekly when one of the sharks bites them. Sharks gotta eat, and the Diva is going to need to be talked off the ledge.

» **The Citizen.** They were raised to follow rules and have great detail orientation. Your organization runs like a third-world open market with no running water or electricity. The first day on the job, they ask you for an operations manual. You truthfully reply, "What's an operations manual?"[5]

Steve Jobs was right. Big strengths (read: extreme assessment scores at either end of a dimension/area) become big weaknesses at times. It's all dependent upon the situation and what you can provide inside that circus you call a company.

Here's Your Golden Profile in Times of High Change

So, I'm telling you that you'll overreact and underreact at the wrong times when seeing assessment scores on candidates you otherwise love.

Is there anything positive I can tell you with certainty? As a matter of fact, there is.

Hiring is a hard-knock life. My time in the field as a talent/selection specialist (remember, I'm a recruiting anthropologist!) has uncovered this important trend:

In high times of change, organizations and hiring managers naturally (and rightfully) migrate to candidates at all levels with *low rules orientation* and *high detail orientation*.

Why is this candidate profile gold in times of high change?

---

5. Bonus points if your alternative reply is, "We don't need no stinking operations manual."

When's the last time you heard someone say the following at your company: "You know what we need? Some more people around here who need to be told exactly what to do and require a LOT of handholding to get things done."[6]

Most companies in a post-pandemic world are in high degrees of flux. Changes to business models, work from home/hybrid situations, and overall disruption place a premium on candidates who can *roll with the punches, go with the flow,* and are *adaptable in chaotic environments.*

Low rules means a candidate won't be alarmed as a new employee when your company is a complete freak show on Day One. They'll figure it out, with or without the company's help, and have a general idea about the best path for them to contribute and add value.

But understanding where they can add value and actually getting it done are two separate things. Having a high-detail orientation dramatically increases the probability they'll actually execute on the things they dream up.

Many companies and hiring managers aren't even aware of their participation in this hiring trend. They're going with their gut, which is hopefully driven by things they've heard in the interview that suggest the candidate will be successful in dealing with change and will get things done in an imperfect environment.

Low Rules + High Details = Ability to Survive and Thrive[7]

When you find this profile in a candidate you like, *just make the hire.*

---

6. Say it in that irresistible Ryan Reynolds way! Also, if you've hired a team that needs this type of guidance, "Beatings will continue until morale improves" is your battle cry.
7. As a final note, nowhere is this hiring trend more applicable than when hiring white-collar, inexperienced/early career professionals. The ability to thrive in change likely also predicts upward mobility in your company as well.

9

What Would You Say You Do Here (Goal Setting)

I found that if you have a goal, that you might not reach it. But if you don't have one, then you are never disappointed. And I gotta tell ya, it feels phenomenal!
—Vince Vaughn as Peter Lafleur in *Dodgeball*

If I wrote a whole book solely about goal setting (too bad I'm not a masochist), it would be called *Just Don't Bore Me*, which is code for the fact that the domain of goal setting is all too often just tedious at best. Managers of people are rarely schooled in what exactly they're supposed to do when it comes to setting goals, so they usually roll out some MBOs or SMART goals and call it a day.

Your team is full of good people. They've got talent and personality, or you wouldn't have hired them. But a funny thing happens once they're in the fold and things start flying at a million miles per hour—*you aren't clear about what the most important things are.* So, they float, you float, and if you're lucky, some meaningful things eventually get done.

The quote from Vince Vaughn to start this chapter underscores the following realities:

» **Goal setting is hard,** or everyone would be perfectly aligned, and they're not.
» **Left to their own devices, humans tend to drift and lose focus.** You don't have to have ADHD to lose sight of what's mission-critical in your job. There are a million things

competing for the attention of your employees. If you don't help them, they're going to be freaking overwhelmed.

» **The only way the situation gets better is by someone leading the process.** Yeah, you could skate by, be average, and not focus on goal setting. But you're better than that, so here we are.

Goal setting isn't easy to do, and it's even harder to pull off in a way that makes your employees feel that you aren't a total bureaucrat. Good thing you've got the skills to deliver.

Fifty Years of Goal-Setting Research Comes Down to This

You want research? Look at the big brain on Brad![1] I thought you'd never ask.

Goal setting has been the topic of research for nearly half a century. That's right, there is an entire set of academics who've chosen (voluntarily) to spend the better part of their professional lives studying this stuff (yikes). That's nuts, right? Over fifty years ago, two dudes named Ed and Gary[2] had a pretty straightforward idea that has held up against all other concepts. They called it *Goal-Setting Theory*, and it goes a little something like this:

> People who set *specific, difficult,* and *observable* goals outperform those who simply "try their best."

Seriously. That's Goal-Setting Theory in a nutshell. Over forty years of research is built on that idea. If you're a super nerd and need it all, the following chart is effective as hell in illustrating everything that goes into making goal setting successful.

---

1. Real recognition from Jules Winnfield (Samuel L. Jackson) to Brad in *Pulp Fiction*. Then he shot the guy.
2. Dr. Edwin Locke and Dr. Gary Latham in "A Theory of Goal Setting and Task Performance." Sexy stuff.

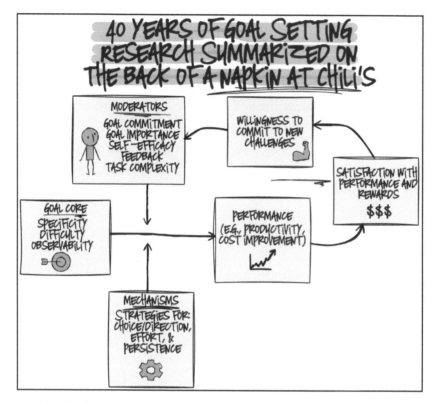

Goal Setting Chart

Note that actually *setting* goals is only 20 percent of the deal. Pesky time-sucks like employee involvement in setting their own goals (I hear you whining) and actually giving on-the-fly coaching and feedback (we'll cover later) are as important as setting the actual goal.

Understand the Opportunity to Be Different When Setting Goals

If you're around a formal goal-setting process in your company, it's fair to say it's likely transactional in nature. You're asked to set goals, so you do, then you rapidly forget them until you're asked to measure whether those goals were actually met.

That's a huge miss for all of us. Rather than going through the motions with goal setting, it's a great time to connect with your direct reports, help give them clarity, and position yourself as the career advocate you are (or want to be).

Simply put, goal setting gives you the opportunity to better connect with the stars in your organization, as well as reach some of the aspirational types who want more from their career. As for the low performers, it gives you something to measure to determine the gaps and figure out what's required to get them where they need to be.

Focus on the Most Important Things for All Your Employees

The Right Number of Goals Is Less Than You Think It Is

Simply put, your employees are dealing with a lot of drama and dumpster fires on a day-to-day basis.

There are a million things that have to get done in any meaningful job. Are all of those things goals? No way. You should reserve formal goals for the most important things that your employees need to contribute for your team, department, and company to be as successful as it possibly can.[3]

There's a lot of research about how many goals you should have active at a given time. The research shows that most people can't reasonably focus on achieving more than three to five goals at any given time. Less is more.

Let's dig into the goal types most likely to make you look like you know what you're doing. Here's what we're covering in our world tour of goal setting: Big Five, SMART goals, MBOs, Burst goals, Developmental goals, BHAG.

---

3. Don't worry, you can always list forty-five things in the job description that some of you freaks also use as a job posting.

SMART GOAL SETTING WORKSHEET				
Specific	Measurable	Achievable	Relevant	Time-Bound
What is your specific goal?	How can you measure this goal?	Is this goal achievable? What resources can you get to make it achievable?	Is this goal important to you? Why?	How long will it take you to achieve this goal? When is the due date?

Goal types

Tool 9: Creating a "Big 5" Set of Goals for Your Direct Reports

Tying Goal Setting to Performance Management in Your Organization

At some point, goal setting has to be connected to how you're going to review performance. As simple as this sounds, lots of organizations miss on this fact.

Many of you work in organizations with *Performance Management/Review Formats* that provide a shell format requiring the manager to insert meaningful goals customized for the position (we talk about this format in greater depth in the Performance Reviews chapter of this book). Goals created for this format become the basis for measuring performance in the job at the end of the year.

When you see this format (and perhaps even if you don't), you should consider using a goal format I call *the Big Five*. Here's the definition of the Big Five goal format:

» The Big Five represents the top five areas for each job in which you have to get results for the employee to meet your expectations.

» The Big Five is the list of the most important things for the employee to focus on.

» Ask yourself this question: If you could only talk about five things/areas of performance with the employee, what would they be? That's the Big Five.[4]

» The Big Five is big-picture goal setting, with room for the employee to figure out how to contribute beyond day-to-day work.

Simply put, you should define the top five areas you need an employee to own, write a statement about what each area is, then define what good versus great (meets/exceeds) performance looks like for each Big Five goal.

Here are a few examples of Big Five items for specific jobs that are written as broad goals without metrics, which come later:

» Develops and manages Lead Generation campaigns that consistently develop qualified leads resulting in sales. (Marketing)

» Develops and oversees our Software Development Process in a manner that consistently produces a product of high quality. (Software Development)

» Maintains high productivity as evidenced by answering high volume of customer calls. (Professional Services/Support)

---

4. All killer, no filler, people.

» Closes out month-end process with high quality and in a timely fashion. (Accounting)[5]

The Big Five isn't a list of things on a job description. It's a short list of the most important ways an employee can impact the business, written as a goal.

Once you have a basic description of the goal, it's time to plug in how you're going to measure whether the employee is meeting or exceeding in the area in question. Here's the Accounting Big Five goal with meets/exceeds targets added to it.

Closes out month-end process with high quality and in a timely fashion. (Accounting)

› **Meets:** Closes month-end process by 12th of each month with limited need for restatement.

› **Exceeds:** Closes month-end process by the 9th of each month with limited need for restatement *and* consistently innovates new tools and reporting features to assist the functional area leaders in running their P&L.

A quick review of this Big Five goal example shows you the value of the format. We've effectively set a "meets" threshold that is measurable, both with the date the books are closed (objective) and limited need for restatements (subjective, manager observation). For exceeds, *it's not enough just to do it quicker*—we're setting the bar higher, by asking for innovation that makes the process better and more usable for the internal clients impacted *in addition* to higher performance in the core area.

Always reserve *exceeds performance* related to goals for value that is added beyond additional raw quantity or quality. That's the

---

5. Is this stuff boring? Maybe. A better question might be "Are you boring?" because once a goal is set, it's kind of your job to bring it to life and make it motivating as a manager of people. It's what happens after a goal is set that really matters.

performance that pushes your team, as well as your direct report, to the next level.

The Big Five format also fits the most smoothly into the coaching model we'll dig into later, as it provides a natural format to contrast good versus great work in any area.[6]

Tool 10: How to Use SMART Goals and MBOs

If you've been a manager of people for more than two years, odds are that someone has told you about *SMART Goals.* If you've been in a big company annual bonus program where at least part of your bonus is based on your performance, odds are you've had an MBO—otherwise known as *Management by Objectives.*

Both SMART goals and MBOs make sense and work as goal types. Let's break them down a bit further:

> **SMART Goals:** SMART stands for Specific, Measurable, Achievable, Relevant, and Time-Bound. Defining these parameters as they pertain to your goal helps ensure that your objectives are attainable within a certain time frame.

Here are a couple of examples of SMART goals to give you a flavor:

» (For a Production Manager) Decrease downtime this year by 20 percent for our three main production lines by hosting weekly meetings with the design manager, materials manager, and production manager to assess where delays are occurring and troubleshoot for improvements.

» (For a Software Development Manager) Scope and perform all approved enhancement requests with an average turnaround

---

6. This format could be called the "coffee for closers" format. Amaze us, high performers of the world!

of twenty business days. Enhancements delivered 99 percent bug-free and clients rate work in this area as "highly satisfied" via survey tool.

These goals are SMART in nature.[7] It's easy to see why the SMART goal format is popular.

What about MBOs? Think of the MBO as the cousin of the SMART goal but often linked to an incentive plan like an annual bonus, more project-based, and often defined more rigidly by deadlines. Here's the broad definition:

> **Management by Objective (MBO) Goals:** A goal set in conjunction with an incentive plan like an annual bonus, designed to define with clarity what an employee needs to accomplish to be eligible for full payment of the incentive.

MBOs are generally used to link individual accomplishments to the incentive plan in question. When used, some companies set incentive plan MBOs annually, but some do it quarterly.

Here are a couple of examples of MBO goals to give you a flavor:

» (For an IT Project Manager) Achieve next HITRUST certification by November 2021, as measured via passing scores on compliance to 550+ controls conducted by External Assessor.
» (For a Marketing Manager) Increase conference registrations by 25 percent by adding weekly email and social media invitations to our partner list and target audiences, refining messaging each week over the three months leading up to the July conference.

---

7. Yeah, I just popped you with SMART Goal examples focused on "downtime" and "turnaround." Can extensive forms I ask you to fill out at the start of the process be far behind?

SMART Goals and MBOs Can Fail to Inspire

SMART Goals and MBOs look pretty similar, right? The biggest issue with the use of SMART goals and MBOs are as follows:

»   They almost always rely on metrics. Not a bad thing, but you don't always have metrics. That's a problem at times, and you start forcing metrics where they really don't fit.

»   They often are time-bound, which means they fade as a mechanism to drive performance once accomplished.

»   They are relatively static, meaning you either hit them or you didn't.

»   Because they are generally yes/no related to achievement of the goal, they don't fit neatly into coaching models designed to contrast good versus great performance. You want great performance, and SMART goals and MBOs don't always promote that.[8]

It's hard to coach direct reports for "exceeds" performance through the use of SMART goals and MBOs. If you love these formats, the pro move is to use a SMART goal to identify "meets" performance, but make sure you show a stretch version of that goal as well as some type of value add/ongoing innovation for "exceeds" level performance (as shown in the Big Five examples).

Burst Goals: Throwing the Struggling
Employee a Life Jacket

We interrupt this high-and-mighty discourse on goal setting to remind you that some of the folks on your team are going to struggle

---

8. It's fair to say that no one ever identified the next great star through a SMART goal or MBO. Stars almost always provide discretionary effort that others don't, and if you have to write it in a goal, it's not discretionary. Word.

at times related to their performance. And if they're struggling with their performance, odds are they aren't meeting the bigger goals you've laid out for them, be they Big Five, SMART, or MBO goals.

Some employees lose their way and need the coaching equivalent of a life jacket and/or a therapy session. When you find yourself with an employee who's flopping around like a fish out of water, Burst Goals are always a good way to get your employee back on track.

> **Burst Goals:** A goal with a small span that supports the achievement of a larger or more complex goal by focusing on the achievement of a specific step in the process of achieving the overall goal.

When your direct report is hyperventilating and can't seem to get anything done, help them break down the insurmountable into smaller parts. Here's the short list of what you get out of Burst Goals:

» **Burst Goals make big things achievable by breaking them up** into smaller, less overwhelming components.
» **Achieving a Burst Goal creates momentum that promotes continued big-goal achievement.** Small wins encourage people to take on the next step with enthusiasm.
» **Burst Goals allow you to track progress** toward achieving larger goals and give you (the manager) a chance to give frequent feedback on progress.

Example of a Burst Goal using our previous Big Five goal from Accounting:

Closes out month-end process with high quality and in a timely fashion (Accounting).

› The *meets* level of performance was "Closes month-end process by 12th of each month with limited need for restatement," but the employee can't seem to hit the deadline.

You ask questions and determine that a good Burst Goal to help them is "Pull all financial data and conduct initial review by the 3rd of each month."

By helping them see the tasks and the timing that have to happen to meet the overall goal, you're giving them counsel to break the bigger goal down into manageable parts.[9]

Most of your Burst Goal conversations will begin in your one-on-one meetings or other coaching conversations. Help struggling employees out with Burst Goals and go coach them up.

Tool 11: Using Developmental Goals Work for Both High and Low Performers

Somewhere along this overly technical journey of goal setting via The Big Five, Smart Goals, and MBOs, you run into a problem/opportunity. The employee needs to grow in a specific area to meet expectations in their current job or to get ready for the next job in their career path.

In both situations, *Developmental Goals* are key.

Development Goals are set during a conversation about what you, as the manager, see as gaps for that direct report given their unique strengths and weaknesses.

The order of the Development Goal process goes like this:

1. You identify gaps and areas in which your direct report needs to improve (to stop sucking in their current job or get ready for what's next).
2. After identifying the area, you tell them why working on the area is good for their career. This is called the WIIFM

---

9. If you have to help an employee with Burst Goals, it's never going to be just one. They're going to need help with multiple Burst Goals to get back on track. Try and ask questions to lead them rather than telling them what to do.

(what's in it for me)—the spoonful of sugar that helps the medicine go down.

Examples of Development Goals at work:

Developmental Barrier: A lack of experience or technical acumen in the area in question.

Angela is a strong accounting manager and wants to run the Finance Department for you but has no experience with financial analysis.

Developmental Goal: Identify forecasting and financial strategy as a skill gap that is essential for Angela's growth. Discuss expanding her current role as accounting manager to include meaningful and specific elements of financial analysis. Commit to providing ongoing feedback about her role expansion. By the end of the year, she will have started to address the skill gap and be better prepared to take on a more expansive role.

BOOM. You've outlined how she needs to prep for where she wants to go. Is it hard telling her that she's at least another year out from her desired role? Sure, it is. But you're both better off if you're straight with her now and help her form the path.[10] If she hits those goals, you'll both have more confidence in her ability to manage the Finance Department.

Angela's development goal is "up with people" because it's pointing to the future. But development goals are needed for those struggling in their current role as well. Consider the case of a dude I'll call "Pete."

Developmental Barrier: Behavior(s) that is limiting that person's effectiveness.

---

10. Real talk. Sometimes, employees think they want a career path, only to get a taste and say, "Wow, that sucks and is not for me." If that is the result of a developmental goal, that's still a huge win.

Pete currently has two direct reports who are very capable; how-ever, Pete never delegates tasks to them. Pete has also complained about his workload and has recently let you know that he wants to manage a larger group (C'mon Pete, really?). On a related note, his current employees have shared that they do not feel chal-lenged by Pete.[11]

This is an opportunity to set a developmental goal around changing that behavior, because Pete's heading for a career car crash if he doesn't fix this.

Developmental Goal: Identify delegating meaningful work to direct reports as a development need. Establish a goal for Pete that directs him to identify two to three meaningful pieces of each project that can be delegated to one or more direct reports and commit to coach them on their progress—both in deliv-ery to deadline and quality of work. By the end of the quar-ter, 35 percent of his workload should be owned by his direct reports.[12]

You've done it again, like the leader you are! That's a goal that will push him into more effective behavioral patterns and set him up to be a more effective manager in the future, which can't be bad for his career. It also prevents you from firing him, which is nice.

Development goals help the business by making employees more effective in their current role. They also prepare employees for the next step in their career by increasing experience and technical acumen or by pushing for behavioral change.

You can't be someone's Best Boss Ever without pushing them via Developmental Goals. Regardless of their status—Natural, Aspirational, or Misfit—there's a Developmental Goal to match their needs.

---

11. Pete's about six months away from not having a job if you can't help him turn it around. A team mutiny is rising!
12. Some of you look at that and say, "So we're supposed to do Pete's job?" Yes. And slowly migrate to him doing it for himself. Sometimes people just need to be shown the example of what *good* looks like.

Once Goals Are Set, They Drive Your Feedback
and Coaching in Multiple Ways

Average managers of people do goal setting to check a box. Great managers of people do goal setting to set up a hundred upcoming conversations in the next year.

When you do goal setting the right way, you've picked the right goal types for the individual employee, and as a result, they know what's expected and also what they need to do to exceed your expectations.

The right goals allow you to use the upcoming coaching and performance feedback tools (later in this book) with authenticity and transparency.

Add your personality and unique conversational flow to the mix and you're well on your way to becoming a Career Agent.

KD'S CHEAT SHEET:
GOAL SETTING

DO THIS!

- Set the right number of goals for your employees. Three to five goals is optimum.
- Tie the goals you set for your employee to your organization's performance management system, if possible.
- Use Burst Goals to help employees who are struggling with bigger goal achievement.
- Create developmental goals that are customized, looking to close skill gaps, or preparing the employee for the next step in their career in accordance with their performance level.
- Require your employees to participate in the goal-setting process.

WATCH OUT FOR THESE TRAPS!

- Don't think all the goals you set with your employee have to have metrics.
- Remember that setting a goal is only the start; your ongoing coaching is critical to helping your direct report achieve their goals.
- Don't set goals that, once accomplished during the year, offer little else for your employee to strive for.
- Avoid being so clinical with goal setting that you don't challenge your highest performers—ensure that goals for this segment of your team are aspirational and career-oriented.

RESOURCES FOR YOU ONLINE - BESTBOSSEVER.ORG

- Additional examples of Big 5, SMART, MBO, Burst, and Developmental Goals.
- Deep tutorials on how to involve your direct report in the goal-setting process, including the set-up for your initial and follow-up meetings until final goals are set
- A methodology for employee involvement in the goal-setting process called "Keep/Toss/Salvage"
- Videos showing manager/employee interaction in the goal-setting process to help you model your approach and talking tracks

MORE FUN STUFF ONLINE

- Video clips on goal setting including Vince Vaughn in *Dodgeball*, Will Smith in *Pursuit of Happiness*, and Jennifer Anniston in *Office Space*

 KRIS DUNN

Elon Musk and the Art of the BHAG

Sometimes, as a leader you have to inspire by thinking big. When you want to think BIG, only one goal type will do.

The BHAG. Otherwise known as a Big, Hairy, Audacious Goal.

BHAGs are visionary strategy statements designed to focus a group of people around a common initiative. They differ from our other goal-setting techniques because BHAGs are positioned toward a large group (rather than individuals) and they typically span a larger amount of time than any of our other goals. They're huge.

BHAGs can come in several flavors. Most are focused on one of four broad categories: reaching a defined target or metric, competition, organizational change, or reputation. Here are a few examples from some companies you've probably never heard of.

- » **Reaching a defined target:** "Attain 1 billion customers worldwide"—Citicorp, 1990s
- » **Competition:** "Crush Adidas"—Nike, 1960s
- » **Organizational change:** "Transform this company from a chemical manufacturer into one of the preeminent drug-making companies in the world"—Merck, 1930s
- » **Reputation:** "Become the company most known for changing the worldwide poor-quality image of Japanese products"—Sony, 1950s

Wait, Nike wasn't always the leader? Japanese products were once considered low quality before Japan started kicking the USA's ass in the 1980s?

Before the world as we know it at Nike and Sony became the reality, leaders at those companies created a BHAG as a single unified vision for their people to rally around.

You know who else is good at BHAGs? Elon Musk. Musk basically BHAG'ed his way into Tesla and SpaceX becoming great companies.

Electric car with quality and luxury? BHAG.

Reusable rockets with segments that can land back on Earth on pads? B-freaking-HAG.

Well, here comes Musk again, probably the most adept user of BHAGs in the world. The ultimate BHAG for him is Mars. More from the *Guardian*:

> Elon Musk has unveiled plans for a new spacecraft that he says would allow his company SpaceX to colonise Mars, build a base on the moon, and allow commercial travel to anywhere on Earth in under an hour. The spacecraft is currently still codenamed the BFR (Big F**king Rocket). Musk says the company hopes to have the first launch by 2022, and then have four flying to Mars by 2024. . . .
>
> The key, he said, was to "cannibalise" all of SpaceX's other products. Instead of operating a number of smaller spacecrafts to deliver satellites into orbit and supply the International Space Station, Musk said the BFR would eventually be used to complete all of its missions. "If we can do that, then all the resources that are used for Falcon9, Dragon, and Heavy can be applied to this system," he said.[1]

1. Michael Slezak and Olivia Solon, "Elon Musk: SpaceX Can Colonise Mars and Build Moon Base," *The Guardian*, September 29, 2017, https://www.theguardian.com/technology/2017/sep/29/elon-musk-spacex-can-colonise-mars-and-build-base-on-oon.

BFR. Musk isn't messing around. The BHAG is set.

Getting NASA astronauts to the International Space Station doesn't happen without the bigger BHAG.

If history tells us nothing else, it tells us that Musk will probably make it happen. Maybe not by 2024, but you can't have a BHAG without making it seem impossible.

You're probably not going to call for a BHAG that morphs an entire industry or colonizes a planet. But the concept of a BHAG can be applied on a smaller scale. Depending on your team type, think of a new product line with a revenue target or a crazy quality/efficiency/production goal.[2]

Your best people want to be inspired. The more stars you have on your team, the more you should be thinking about your version of the BHAG to keep them interested and engaged.[3]

---

2. Real talk: You having a BHAG for your team is a great way to look different than other managers. Just saying.
3. BHAGs for stars on your team directly align with being a Career Agent for your people. Better retention of stars follows because they're being stretched and doing interesting work.

10

Did I Just See You Viciously Mock Your Coworker Again?
(Coaching Skills)

*A coach is someone who can give correction
without causing resentment.*
—John Wooden

2:21 p.m. on Wednesday

Class A Office Space (subleased) in a top 20 metropolitan statistical area (MSA)

"I just don't know what they're thinking and wanted you to know."

Drop-by Steve had walked in the door two minutes ago, doing what he does best. Sharks gotta swim, shooters gotta shoot.

Death. Taxes. Steve informally walking in my office for a chat that could last anywhere from five to forty-one minutes. Nothing, it seems, could wait for our one-on-one.

Steve was a talented guy (HR manager) who worked for me a couple of companies ago. Energetic and expressive, he had some diva in him and had to be talked down from the ledge at times when executives and managers he served played rough and he thought it was an affront to our company culture and his capability.[1] Turns out, most were just jerks of the narcissistic ilk.

---

1. That would be high sensitivity, friends. He needed more hugs than his internal client group was willing to provide.

But wait! Our conversation on this day was wrapping up! Was I about to get back to my day after a mere six minutes with Steve? Was he dropping out as quickly as he dropped in?

It was true. He said thanks and walked out the door. But 20 seconds after he left, Steve interrupted my Outlook reimmersion period[2] as he reemerged, poked his head in my door, and asked a question I'll never forget.

"You just used the thing on me, didn't you?"

"Yes I did," was my reply as I made one second of eye contact with him before returning my gaze to my monitor with a slight s**t-eating grin.[3] Steve laughed out loud and was gone.

Drop-by Steve had just been handled by, arguably, the most important hack in any manager's arsenal: informal coaching, delivered on-the-fly, with no consequences.

When used well, the best leadership tools can't be distinguished from normal conversation.

You've Been Hit By . . . A Smooth Criminal

Steve had been the target of one of the smoothest, stealthiest tools available to managers of people: the *Six-Step Coaching Tool*, also known as Drive-By Coaching, On-The-Fly Coaching, or the Jedi Mind Trick by those who love it and deploy it on the unsuspecting masses.

The Six-Step Coaching Tool doesn't force managers to stop the world, schedule a meeting, and stiffen up to deliver hard feedback to direct reports in need. Those meetings suck. Instead, I'm going to suggest in this chapter that you should lighten the hell up on your formal coaching meetings (always delivered too late, BTW)

---

2. Patent pending. My next book is how to return to Outlook Zen after being interrupted by a drop-in.
3. Always return your eyes to the monitor when someone returns for "one last question," even while answering.

and instead offer coaching for improvement on a daily basis when you see the need.

"*Thanks, Captain Obvious,*" you say. I get it. I'm not offering Dalai Lama–level depth on my insight here. But for every one hundred people who read this book, ninety-nine have no clue whatsoever about the best way to get into that coaching conversation on the same day, much less the same moment, that they see the need.

So, what do those ninety-nine people do? They wait and don't coach when they need to. Pretty soon, they're rationalizing reasons they don't coach, like "Ben's always bitchy and defensive during budget forecast meetings: that's just Ben." Could Ben have made a simple change if you had engaged the first time you saw the bitchiness? Of course he could. But you delayed, and now you're attributing behavior to how Ben's parents raised him: bitchy-**s Ben.[4]

That's what the tool is for. Memorize six simple steps and start engaging on a same-day basis. You'll be amazed at what happens, and direct reports will simply think you're helping them troubleshoot, like any good Career Agent should. I smell rising engagement scores delivered to you by a mystified HR business partner.

The Middle Is Where the Coaching Relationship and Impact Is Located

No matter how much lipstick leadership gurus put on books, seminars, and TED talks, there are basically three times when you coach your employees:

» When things are good (**the easy part!**).
» When things could be better, but it's not a crisis—yet (**the "you're avoiding this" part!**).

---

4. Actual person. We used to wonder if the behavior was allowed at the dinner table by his weak parents.

» **When things are so bad, it's absolutely a crisis.** So much so you're putting the employee in question in some type of formal process at your company, and they won't be at your company if they don't turn it around. (Easier for most managers than number two!)

This section is all about the middle: the gray area. The things that go bump in the night. The times when you see things that definitely need correction, but it's not a crisis yet. You just need your direct report to understand that there's a better way, and you have to guide them there.

As Don Draper once said to a direct report in *Mad Men*, "That's what the money is for!"[5]

Make Your Definition of Coaching Micro Instead of Macro

Coaching can be a complete corporate buzzword. You don't have time for buzzword noise or highbrow leadership principles. With that in mind, let's start this by throwing you my definition of coaching:

> **Coaching** is a dialogue between manager and employee on any component of performance that's in need of a tweak.

Sounds simple enough, right? Let's deconstruct my definition to point out that the coaching opportunities are everywhere around you, and if you're not engaging multiple times a day, you're probably doing it wrong. Let's dig in to the definition with the following color commentary:

» **Dialogue between manager and employee.** Simply put, *coaching is a conversation* between the manager and the direct report.

---

5. Draper yelled this at a direct report when she complained about him taking credit for her ideas. He was smoking and drinking as he delivered this encouragement. The feedback environment could have been better.

It's not enough to give feedback and run. Coaching, when done right, involves the manager doing most of the listening and the employee doing most of the talking, or at least a 50/50 split. Simply put, if they don't talk, you can't win.

So you should SHUT UP more than you think. But that doesn't mean you have to block off lots of time. Usually, you can accomplish what's needed in five minutes or less. Let's break down the simple definition of coaching a bit more:

» **Any component of performance.** Coaching conversations are focused around things that are directly and indirectly tied to performance. Coaching can also be centered around behaviors that influence an employee's development and career path. If it's within the realm of work, you can (and should) use your coaching skills to improve current performance.

» **Tweaks.** I love this word when it comes to coaching because a tweak is micro in nature. It can mean doing less of something. It can also mean doing more of something. The tweaks available with employees are everywhere around you; the only limiting factor is focus, having a lightweight coaching framework to use, and the will to kick a little butt every day.

Add it all up, and it begs the question: Are you coaching enough? Most of us aren't, and even if you feel you are, you likely have opportunities to get better outcomes.

Let's dig in.

Tool 12: The Six-Step Coaching Tool for Daily Coaching
The Only Coaching Tool You'll Ever Need to Be Awesome

Why don't we coach more than we do? Simple. Confrontation sucks.

As humans, most of us hate to confront others. If you're uncomfortable with confrontation and aren't sure how to get into the conversation, the first thing you'll do is avoid the talk. We also avoid coaching conversations because we don't want to rock the boat. We just want the person to get the work done on time without drama. Coaching feels like drama to most of us.

The problem, of course, is that if you don't get in there and coach daily, you're getting tire-tracked by the world,[6] used and abused by the machine, and accepting outcomes for you and your people you don't have to accept.

We feel your pain. That's why we're giving you a tool that can wrap up most coaching conversations in five minutes or less. It can be used for any coaching situation that falls short of needing a formal process or progressive discipline. If you spend more than five minutes coaching with this tool, you've got an opportunity to be more efficient with your coaching. If you spend more than ten minutes with an employee when using this tool, you may like to hear yourself talk.

This tool is uber-simple. The simple-to-memorize sequence of The Six-Step Coaching Tool breaks down like this:

1. State what you specifically observed (or what technology or others have observed).
2. Wait for a response. This is where you *shut up*.
3. Tell them why it matters.
4. Ask questions about what they can do differently next time and *shut up again*.[7]
5. Agree together.
6. Close upbeat!

I provided the six steps without commentary so you could see how simple it is. Got it?

---

6. Definition of *tire-tracked*: Not taking action and allowing the world to determine you can be run over, at which point the world stops respecting you and sends you the worst possible outcomes on a weekly, if not daily, basis.
7. Yes, I'm asking you to shut up twice. Because I know you just want to tell them what to do.

Let's give you a little more depth on each step:

» **State what you or others have observed.** You're simply saying
what you've seen in this step, nothing more—no judgment, no
troubleshooting—just an observation. For best results, use a
specific example that happened recently to reinforce a broader
trend. Keep it to thirty seconds max on your intro here, and
we'd prefer it to be fifteen seconds or less.

  › Where You'll Mess It Up: You'll speak in glittering generalities without making a clear, simple statement that
  qualifies as a single observation, and because of that, you'll
  wax poetic and drag on for two to three minutes. They'll
  have no idea what you're talking about. Just give it to them
  straight. You may feel like a jerk, but that's okay—you're
  not used to the tool yet.

  › Example: *"John, I saw you interrupt Peggy in our meeting
  again"* (let's say John is a marketing manager working for
  you, and Peggy is the director of customer service).

» **Wait for a response.** This is where you shut up. After delivering your observation, stop talking and wait for a response. This
step can be the toughest, especially with a quiet team member,
but don't bail them out.[8] That limits the effectiveness of your
session and your ongoing coaching relationship. You may need
to help the team member with a "bridge" if they don't respond.

  › Where You'll Mess It Up: The most common mistake for a
  coaching rookie is that you talked so much in Step #1 you
  went ahead and told them what to do, which means there's
  no chance for employee involvement or the true accountability that comes along with it. So, you stop talking and the
  employee's basically thinking, "You told me what to do . . .
  now what do you want me to say?"

---

8. For practice, when someone asks you a question next week, wait twenty seconds before responding and feel the burn. Awkward.

› Example of Employee Response (John, after you refused to do more than make your simple observation): *"Yeah, Peggy drives me crazy, she has no context for how busy other people are; it's always about her."* [9]

» **Tell them why it matters.** Once your direct report has responded, be ready to remind them of the goals in the coaching area you are focused on. Rehearsal is key in this area—don't neglect precoaching preparation (it should take two minutes to prep before you use this tool) and have an idea what you want to say. Focus not only on the goals for the team member but also on how those goals are aligned with the overall goals of your department and team.

› Where You'll Mess It Up: The biggest challenge with Step #3 is that you'll automatically migrate from reminding them of the goals in the area in question to telling them what to do to fix the issue. You can't do that. Your employee needs to come up with the ideas. Another challenge to this step of our coaching tool is that you'll sound like a complete robot. Don't use buzzwords.

› Example (talking to John): *"Yeah, I know that we all have people who get under our skin, but we need a good relationship with Peggy to get everything done that's on our plate this year. When you battle with her, it hurts the rest of us."*

» **Ask questions about what they can do differently next time and shut up again.** This is the second time in the coaching tool where you force the person to talk. They need to come up with at least some of the ideas on how to fix the situation in front of you, no matter how minor. Be prepared to follow up and lightly prompt them if they struggle to come up with ideas.

› Where You'll Mess It Up: Instead of just asking questions, you'll lead the witness again. As soon as you intro with

---

9. John could literally say, "I saw Peggy stealing computers from the office" or "I've been crashing at Peggy's house after benders" and we're still going to make it through the six steps of the coaching tool. #discipline

things like "could you . . ." or "maybe the best thing . . ." you're screwed. Asking open-ended questions forces the employee to come up with some of the solutions. Don't worry, if their solutions are awful, you're not rolling with them, but you have to give them a chance.

› Example: *"What can you do differently moving forward to better meet the goal?"* or better yet, go informal: *"What can you do differently the next time Peggy aggravates you in a meeting so you don't kill the rest of us?"*

» **Agree together.** After you ask questions in Step #4 and get reactions from the employee, this is a closing statement on what you agree to do moving forward: a summary delivered by the manager (you). You're going for closure and seeking agreement from the team member regarding changes they're going to make.

› Where You'll Mess It Up: You don't position your phraseology as a question. Instead, you'll tell them what you heard and assume it's been agreed to. You have to phrase it as a question and make them agree to it—a small tweak that matters behaviorally.

› Example: *"So, we agree moving forward that when Peggy's talking, instead of interrupting her you're going to take notes in your notebook and wait for a natural breaking point in the group conversation to share your thoughts, correct?"*[10]

» **Close upbeat!** The best managers of people close any coaching session on a high note, which is you weaving the agreement together with your belief in the employee's ability to do the job. Think of it as a positive, soft close to feedback for improvement.

› Where You'll Mess It Up: You're enough of a robot at this stage that you'll just say "thanks." Wherever the employee is in the spectrum of performance, you've got to have an upbeat close that's personalized enough to be meaningful.

---

10. Alternatively, "We agree you'll make eye contact with me if I'm in the room and blink twice because you feel danger."

> Example: *"Alright, alright, alright. Thanks for talking to me about that. You do great work but I wouldn't be your partner if I didn't push you to stop shooting your own foot. I'm glad you're on my team."* [11]

Tool 13: How to Deal with Coaching Sidetracks from Your Employees
It Wasn't Me: The Sidetracks You'll Encounter from Your People and How to Kill Them

This just in: coaching conversations are rarely smooth. People are people, and they generally have a hard time admitting when they have room for improvement. When you coach, there may be grinding of teeth, rubbing of hands, bad body language, and general loathing of your existence.

Denial: Not just a river in Egypt.

In fact, if you're using my coaching tool and you get all the way through it exactly as planned, one of two things may be happening:

» The person you're coaching may be deferring to you based on your positional authority and might even be a bit scared of you,[12] or

» The person you're coaching did the minimum necessary to get out of the conversation as quickly as possible. Generally by agreeing with you, they planned to get you to STFU as soon as possible.

It's not a great outcome either way. If your direct report engages, expect them to whine. Expect them to moan, with finger pointing probable as well. All of this is part of the process.

---

11. Only managers with five to ten years of experience can credibly use the Matthew McConaughey intro to this step.
12. Also scary is the fact you're making an observation about them and then shutting up. What's that about?

When coached, your direct reports will try to blame others or factors outside of their control. These deflections are called *Sidetracks* and are designed to get you to abandon your will to coach: aka destroy your coaching game.

The primary flavors of Sidetracks are as follows (I dare you not to grin, curse, or shake your head in agreement when you hear these):

» **What about them?** Ah yes, the Sidetrack you'll see the most and love to hate. This deflection clearly states that other people are struggling and perhaps have the same issues. Why don't you go away and deal with them, big shot?

» **What about you?** Whoops! S**t just got real. In this Sidetrack, your employee is saying that you're part of the problem—not giving them what they need, not following up on things you committed to and more. This one's personal, and can be delivered softly or harshly, but the message is clear—you're to blame. Why do you suck so much?[13]

» **My tools stink.** Yes! I could do better, but the resources I have at my disposal clearly aren't up to snuff. Please end this coaching session now, as there's no way I can be successful with the tool set that's been transported back from the 1980s to assist me.

» **The customer stinks.** This deflection calls out problematic clients and customers as the reason for the performance struggle on which you're coaching your direct report. The world is full of tough customers, and it's easy to have Stockholm syndrome with your employees when it comes to this Sidetrack.

» **My life stinks.** From the tragic (terminally ill family member) to the serious (financial problems) to the WTF (partner just ran off with personal trainer), it's hard to continue a coaching session with employees who share life struggles with you as a reason for not hitting the performance bar in any area. But continue you must.

---

13. Happens most often when the employee is more assertive than you are as a manager. They're trying to bully you.

» **<Insert any other Sidetrack you can think of here>.** My list isn't all-inclusive. You'll hear other Sidetracks that don't neatly fit into the aforementioned categories. Recognize them for what they are, and get back to the steps in the coaching tool.

I know. The gall. *The nerve of these people with their Sidetracks.*

Your job as the coach when you hear a Sidetrack as a reason for the performance struggle? Put all the sidetracks and emotional reactions to the side. Deal with and deflect the Sidetracks, so you can get back to what's real—the change you need to see in your employee to make them as good as they can be.

Remember, some of these Sidetracks are 100 percent real. But you can't solve the world's problems in your coaching session. For best results, do the following:

» **Be empathetic if there is truth to the Sidetrack.** It's okay to acknowledge they might be right. *"Yeah, that sucks."*

» **Offer to knock down a barrier or two to assist.** But don't do that and stop coaching. Say that you'll help if you can, but continue with the coaching tool. *"I'll see if I can help on that, but regardless of whether that help comes, what can you do differently?"*

» **Focus them on what they can control when asking for next steps toward improvement.** Sure, there are other people with the same problem, the tools are imperfect, and the customer is difficult. Whatever you're coaching them on, ask for what they can do differently via what they control to get better results. *"What can you do differently given what you can control?"*

Sidetracks are generally presented to you in Step #2 (when they respond to your initial observation) or Step #4 (when you ask them what they can do differently) of the Six-Step Coaching Tool. Use one of more of these strategies and keep bringing them back to the coaching tool and what they can control.

Nobody said it would be simple. But you're good enough, smart enough, and gosh darn it, some people actually like you.[14]

Coaching Positive Work Isn't the Hard Part, Skippy
Coaching Is Linked to Everything Else in Your Manager Toolbox

We wrap up this tour de force of coaching skills with an acknowledgment that we haven't talked much about *coaching positive work*.

Coaching positive work is the recess of your life as a manager.[15] When you see good work, say it. Say it directly to the person in the moment, and share with others in meetings and across your comms platforms (email, Slack, etc.) that the person is crushing it. If you need multiple chapters on this topic, you've bought the wrong book.

Coaching on the fly for small improvements, on the other hand, is not just part of the game, *it is the game*. There's nothing that can position you as Career Agent better than informal conversations designed to make your direct report better. Mix positive coaching with coaching for improvement at a 3:1 ratio, and you're on your way.

You saw something today that, if addressed and engaged on, could make your direct report better and more successful in the future.

What the hell are you waiting on?

---

14. The more you can memorize the steps of the tool, the more you'll sound like you when you're live, which means you'll get better results via authenticity.
15. Other things that are easy and you do daily: eating bad food, watching TV instead of walking or going for a run, etc. So why wouldn't you provide recognition more than you do? It's literally the victory lap of your life as a manager.

KD'S CHEAT SHEET:
COACHING SKILLS

DO THIS!

- Memorize the six simple steps of the coaching tool so you don't have to look at a page when you're live with an employee.
- Get at least 10 repetitions in with your employees using the tool of small tweaks for improvement. Take notes on what you learned and where you struggled. Get better the next time in that area.
- Look for opportunities to use the coaching tool daily moving forward.
- Coach at least one time a day using the tool.
- As you get comfortable with the tool, become less stiff and talk like you normally talk. Authenticity is the key, and you want coaching conversations to feel as normal as possible for best results.

WATCH OUT FOR THESE TRAPS!

- Don't think you have to schedule a meeting with an employee to coach them on a topic.
- Don't make your initial observation more than fifteen seconds long.
- Don't tell the employee in front of you what they should do. They need to come up with the ideas, and if you need to nudge them to brainstorm in a certain area, do that. But don't tell them what they should do.
- Don't get blown up by a Sidetrack about others, tools or difficult clients/customers. Get to the next step in the Six-Step Coaching Tool.

RESOURCES FOR YOU ONLINE - BESTBOSSEVER.ORG

- Cheat sheet showing the Six-Step Coaching Tool you can print out as a reference
- Sidetrack reference card to build resilience prior to your coaching session

MORE FUN STUFF ONLINE

- Coaching videos including Kristen Bell from *House of Lies* and Brad Pitt in *Moneyball*

 KRIS DUNN

Bonus

Coaching Your Ambitious Direct Report Not to Be Hated

If you're like me, you love a direct report with ambition.[1]

People with ambition get s**t done. Do they get things done because they believe in you as a leader, or they believe in themselves?

If you're asking that question, you're concerned with the wrong things. Just celebrate the execution that comes with raw ambition and stop thinking so much. (The answer, by the way, is that they believe in themselves and are motivated by moving their careers forward.)

One problem that is universal in relation to direct reports with high ambition levels is that they can become hated by their peers—the folks they work with. It's pretty simple to see why. The folks with ambition treat life like a scoreboard and are often "low-team" (motivated by an individual scoreboard rather than team scoreboards). Their peers, on the other hand, want to do good work, but for the most part don't have designs to rule the world.

Friction ensues. The team views the high-ambition direct report like an opportunistic freak. A brown-noser. Someone who would run over his own mother for the next promotion.

So, how do you coach your *high-ambition direct report* to play nice with the lower-ambition locals?

The key in my experience is to confront the reality with the high-ambition direct report: *You're looking to do great things. You're driven. You want to go places and you're willing to compete with anyone you need to in order to get there.*

Start with that level set. Celebrate it. Hug it out.

---

1. Unless they want your job. I kid. Or do I?

Then tell the driven person in front of you that you need something from them.[2] They have to get purposeful with recognition of their peers.

If a high-ambition direct report starts a weekly, informal pattern of recognition of their peers, a funny thing happens. They start to look human to those around them.

But in order to make it work, you have to confront the ambitious one(s) and convince them that work life is not a zero sum game—just because they give kudos to someone else doesn't mean the high-ambition FTE won't get the promotion or the sweet project assignment from you.

It actually makes them stronger, because in addition to all the great individual work they do, they start to be perceived as a good-to-great teammate, which unlocks some doors to management/leadership roles in a way that great individual work can't.

But that doesn't happen for the high-ambition direct report unless you are honest with them about this:

1. You're high ambition and would run over your grandpa to win/survive/advance.[3]
2. Your peers think you're a d*ck, and that's going to limit you.[4]
3. You're going to fix it by recognizing those around you on a weekly basis for great work, and you're going to reinforce that recognition by sharing your thoughts informally beyond the email you send, the shout out you make in a meeting, etc.

Tell your high-ambition direct report to stop being a jerk. Ask them to share the love, and they'll actually get to where they want to go sooner.

---

2. The really smart and aware ones saw this feedback sandwich coming. Probably because they just rattled someone's cage the day before.
3. Potentially empathizing that grandpa had it coming as a part of this conversation is a style choice you'll have to make as a leader.
4. Insert gender appropriate, illustrative words here as needed. But to make them hear you, you'll have to be 100 percent honest and forceful. Don't beat around the bush; tell them how they're viewed at times in their drive to win.

11

There Are Actually a Lot of Bad Ideas in Brainstorming

(Managing Change)

Running a startup is like eating glass. You start to like the taste of your own blood.

—Sean Parker, cofounder of Napster

Your company (and career) exists in an industry that is changing. The question is whether you're doing the work to explore what's next or simply protecting the way things have always been.

Let's talk about the music industry. If you're over forty years of age, you grew up with music delivered in a format that's different than what we know today. Depending on how old you are, you may have been a part of four different music formats preceding streaming that housed the beats/riffs of your favorite hair band or profane rap group (albums, 8-track tapes, cassette tapes, CDs).[1]

While competition has always been fierce in the music industry, the flagship providers in the business always controlled one important aspect of their business: *distribution.*

Until they didn't. That's when things got tricky. *What's up, Napster?*

Change came in the form of a disruptive pirate ship named Napster, founded by a kid named Shawn Fanning. Napster created a disruptive product that allowed for peer-to-peer sharing—meaning

---

1. Boomers have shoeboxes of 8-tracks from their youth; Gen X has cassette tapes. Don't hate them due to history.

you could put your whole music library online from your PC—and I could download songs from you—without paying anyone.[2]

It was kind of a big deal. Of course, the music industry fought it, but the damage was done and music would never be the same, as evidenced by the total revenue chart for the industry shown here.

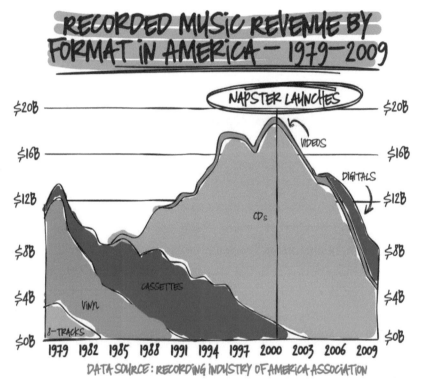

RECORDED MUSIC REVENUE BY FORMAT IN AMERICA — 1979–2009

NAPSTER LAUNCHES

DATA SOURCE: RECORDING INDUSTRY OF AMERICA ASSOCIATION

Looking back, technology made almost frictionless delivery modes for music possible. Of course, Napster and related services like LimeWire were ultimately illegal (Gen X sad face) and, for the most part, didn't survive.

But Napster gave way to iTunes and digital cigarette-pack-sized iPods, and some people thought Apple had won forever. But that obviously was a shortsighted prediction.

---

2. The baller move during this time was to find someone with similar tastes on Napster and download their entire library.

More technology changes (specifically wireless broadband) morphed the advantage of streaming over downloads (Spotify).[3] You have to expect something else will follow, driven by more change. Change happens, with similar stories of fat cats protecting legacy cash-cow advantages at Blockbuster, Eastman Kodak, Motorola, and RIM Blackberry.[4]

You probably don't have the opportunity to prevent a similar big strategic misstep at your company. But that doesn't mean you can't be great at change. You just have to chase change with a small "c" rather than a capital "C."

Tool 14: The Change Agile Cycle
You Don't Have to Own Nine Hoodies to Innovate and Drive Change

You're not Shawn Fanning. You've got a real job, a real team, and a notably substandard selection of hoodies. You're not in the market to bootstrap the next piece of software that's going to destroy/steal/reallocate billions of dollars of revenue from an unsuspecting industry.

But you're 100 percent on the hook to manage change at your company and to disrupt some s**t while you're at it.

There's broken stuff everywhere around you. Your team, while not expecting it to be you, is looking for a hero. They see the dysfunction, the broken processes, the things that don't work, and they wish someone had the guts and skill to challenge it all.

What about you? You could be the one to try and fix some things. The PhDs will try and overwhelm you with change management principles/methodologies and basically make you afraid of trying to make a difference.

---

3. Let's mess with the minds of Gen Z here and reveal that we used to pay 10 cents per text sent as well.
4. I know a boomer who still uses a Blackberry; I call him Rex (short for T-Rex), and his wife hates me for it.

I'm going to give you a simple process to work on change. Let's take a look at the *Change Agile Cycle*.

The Change Agile Cycle is a methodology that follows agile development in the software industry (more hoodies), where requirements for minimum viable products (MVPs) are written, and products/features are designed, developed, and tested. If the data that comes back validates success, the feature is released. If the data from testing is bad, the MVP is either abandoned or sent back to the team for rework and subsequent relaunch.

Fail fast is the motto.[5]

Simply put, change that involves innovation isn't point-to-point, it's a process that looks like a wheel. The Change Agile Cycle I recommend to work problems—big and small—appears here.

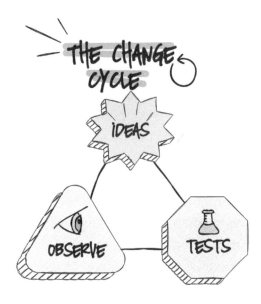

Here are your cliff notes on what each one of the stages means (we'll talk about each stage in the sections that follow):

1. **Observe:** You can't do change or improvement, big or small, without having data that tells you there's a problem.

---

5. A good rule to live by. Also, "Get busy living or get busy dying," via Andy Dufresne from *Shawshank Redemption*.

You have no shortage of these! They're everywhere in your organization.

2. **Ideas:** Once you have some observations about the problem you're facing, you're ready to create ideas that could be fixes. Think of ideas as potential fixes you whiteboard out in brainstorm mode, keeping in mind cost and impact to your organization. Nothing's free.

3. **Tests:** Once you've selected an idea to fix the problem and made sure the solution is as small as you can make it (while still having impact), it's time to launch a test. A test is created, you go live with the change, and establish a set period you'll run it for. Data and observations are gathered from the test, which guides you to a Pursue/Pivot/ Abandon decision.

Think of the Change Agile Cycle as a building block of change at all levels—like a molecule, atom, or DNA strand. No matter how big and complex your change need becomes, keep coming back to this cycle as a method to increase your speed, reduce your risk, and above all else, help you and your team look like killers and better than the competition (whether you define that as external or internal).[6]

How to Determine What You Want to Put into the Change Agile Cycle

Great managers of people are nimble. They understand that maximizing performance of the team and protecting/promoting the careers of their people requires them to be agile AF.

Simply put, if you're waiting for someone else to tell you to make things better, you're already the Kodak film camera of your company—you just don't know it yet.

---

6. Yes, you want to help the company get better. You also want to outperform your peers. Never forget the game inside the game.

Change opportunities with a small "c" (meaning you call the shots, you don't need anyone's approval) are everywhere around you, including the following gems:

» **Broken processes.** I heard you had a few. Feels like something you could deliver on.
» **Customer needs.** These are gaps in what your company does for clients, just waiting for you to impact via Change Agile and add a decimal point or two on the Net Promotor Score (NPS) report.
» **Challenging the status quo.** Just asking the question "why?" or "why do we do it like that?" when something obviously sucks is solid change agent behavior.
» **Growth/innovation/new product opportunities.** When you run out of obvious things to fix, change can get fun via the whole "what's next?" vibe. Chasing new things is sure to keep your best people engaged as they have a chance to learn new things, flex strengths, and generally go after world domination.[7]

If it all sounds like too much work, I feel bad for you. You don't like what you do and are a complete drag to be around. But odds are if you're reading this book, you like challenges.

Pro tip: You only have so many change projects you can onboard while you do your day job. Keep no more than three change projects in the portfolio on the team (or one active per each direct report), and actually ship/finish one before you add the next one.

When you're the hammer, everything looks like a nail. Slow and steady, champ.

---

7. Please start slow and fix a thing or two that's broken before you start whipping out terms like "innovation."

Tool 15: The Idea Evaluator
How to Run Brainstorming Sessions without Getting Hijacked by Horrible Ideas

So you have a target for the Change Agile Cycle: something broken that needs fixing. Do you know how to fix it? Stop right there. To get the buy-in needed from your team, you're going to have to brainstorm ideas and solutions to that problem and let them participate. It takes a village.

Many of you have guided your team through a brainstorming session before.[8] At the end of it, you have a list of ideas. *For best results in Change Agile, use sticky notes that can be moved around a flip chart sheet.*

What's next after you collect all the ideas? You could go one of three ways, with two of the following options being wrong:

» You could let the mob decide what to do. Bad idea.
» You could tell the mob what you're going to do. Worse idea. Who are you, Mussolini?[9]
» You could have an adult conversation about the best idea to pursue given the combined cost and value of each idea.

Can you guess which one is the right strategy? My use of the seminegative term "mob" (shout-out to Rome) and references to fascists are designed to point you in the right direction.

The preferred next step is to evaluate the ideas that have been generated via a process called the *Idea Evaluator*. Simply put, you're going to create another flip chart and lead another round of facilitation that allows your team to determine the cost/value tradeoffs of each idea. When you're done interacting with the team, your flip chart will look something like the chart below.

---

8. Underrated skill: Looking energized by a brainstorming idea from a direct report you'd like to laugh at.
9. My go-to, low-risk fascist/socialist reference. Will the reference get this book banned from SHRM in 2029? Perhaps.

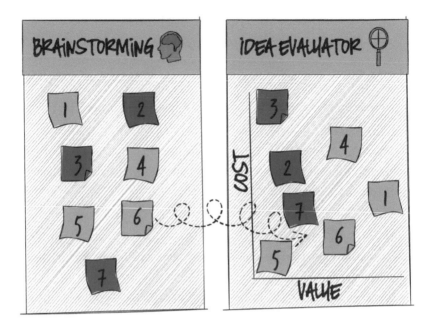

Here are some notes to help you facilitate process and work your team through each idea and plot it via the Idea Evaluator:

» **Cost:** What's the investment (money or resource time) needed to make the Idea in question happen? What resources are involved? How big of a distraction is the change to day-to-day work and responsibilities?

» **Value:** What type of bang for your buck do you get if the Idea is successfully implemented? Big solutions are great, but they come with more cost, which is why we do the yin-yang plotting of cost versus value.

Pro tip: Force all to participate. If you know an error is being made in plotting on the cost/value chart, ask smart questions to lead the team back to what's real.[10] Remember, you're leading this process to get buy-in on the work that's about to come.

---

10. Word track: "How's everyone feel about the idea for our plumbing company to take a stand against climate change? Low value to the business? Kind of broad?"

The awesome thing about this process is you don't have to tell someone their idea sucks. The team kills them with kindness and a *Lord of the Flies*–like plotting of their idea on the cost versus value grid.

Good times.

Tool 16: The Influencer Map of Change
Avoid the Red Wedding with This Political Tool

Damn, you really did it. You identified something that needed to be fixed, brainstormed with your team, came up with your top solution, and are almost ready to start building and testing the solution. Nicely done!

We interrupt this session on getting things done and making things better to remind you of the Red Wedding. The Red Wedding happened to Robb and Catelyn Stark in *Game of Thrones*, when they thought everything was cool with a jilted rival family and attended a wedding, only to be brutally gutted and killed. They never saw it coming.[11]

When you pursue change, it's wise to map out potential obstacles to ensure you don't walk into your own corporate version of the Red Wedding. Map out your risk with the *Influencer Map of Change*, which lets you think about who is a *supporter* and who is a *blocker*. To create this map, simply do the following:

» List your idea/proposed change in a box in the bottom left corner.

» Draw a diagonal line from that box to the upper right corner, label it "Neutral."

---

11. This never would have happened if Ned Stark was alive. Of course, Ned also had issues with reading the room.

» Add "Very Supportive" in the upper left corner and "Less Supportive" in the bottom right corner.[12]

» Using sticky notes for each individual or department, discuss and place them on the continuum between Very Supportive/ Neutral/Less Supportive. Each person/department will fall on a range from the upper left corner to the bottom right corner. Once you determine that, move those most impacted by the change closer to the lower left corner, and those less directly impacted by the change toward the upper right corner.

Creating the Influencer Map in this manner allows you to visualize who your supporters/early adopters will be and also to understand who you need to approach in order to ask for support before the idea/change is deployed. See the chapter on "Framing" later in this book for a master class in proactive communications during times of change.

Of course, sometimes begging for forgiveness beats asking for permission. But the more your organization feels like *Game of Thrones*, the more you need to use this tool. It's always nice to know who's coming with the dagger.

Tool 17: How to Test Ideas in the Change Agile Cycle
Calling Dr. Kevorkian

The last stage of the Change Agile cycle is testing ideas. I'm including a tool called the *One Page Change Worksheet* in the web resources for this chapter, which will help you line up what needs to be done to prep the idea you're testing, go live with the change, and evaluate the outcomes. Go download that worksheet to track the testing of any idea you've selected.

There are two core concepts in testing ideas in Change Agile:

---

12. Alternative titles for these sections: "Fans" and "Will try and end my career at least two times in Q4 alone for this process power grab."

» **Minimum viable product (MVP).** Don't overengineer the idea you want to test. Instead, test the idea with just enough features to gather validated learning about the change and its continued development. This makes your test less expensive than working a change with more features, which increases cost and risk that the change will fail due to incorrect assumptions.[13]

» **Use of a hypothesis.** I know, it sounds nerdy as hell. But a hypothesis is just a simple statement on what the test is, like this:

> Our team expects by <change description>, we will <solve this problem>, which will have <list benefits> as measured by <this measurement>.

In other words, don't build things you don't need when testing ideas.

Get in and out and look to answer the question if the test worked or not in weeks, not months. Smart, agile/lean managers (that's you, BTW) review all active changes tests at least monthly (every two weeks is better) and decide to pursue, pivot, or abandon the change:

» **Pursue** means that the idea (for our consideration, the change) worked and we should keep doing similar things. This would lead to building on this idea to make it slightly more complex or launching other tests that are related to the initial concept.

» **Pivot** means that the idea kind of worked, but it needed a bit of tweaking. In this case, you'd keep what worked and slightly modify the MVP and reintroduce it in the testing cycle.

» **Abandon** means that the idea (change) didn't work. We don't keep doing this one; we kill it, learn from it, and develop other tests with learning in mind.

---

13. Perfect is the enemy of good. Your team is going to want to build more. Be the adult, say no, and ship simple.

Brainstorm, select the idea you want to test, and launch it. Kill it faster than ABC killed the TV series *Cavemen* if it doesn't work.[14]

Make change part of your game and differentiation as a manager of people.

KD'S CHEAT SHEET: CHANGE MANAGEMENT

DO THIS!

○ Find things that are broken around your department.
○ Brainstorm ideas that could fix them. Lead a team session to grade all ideas on a cost/value scale.
○ Pick an idea, don't overengineer it, and clearly define how it's going to be tested, measured, and launched.
○ Evaluate progress: pursue, pivot, or abandon.
○ Have three ideas for change in play across your team at all times using the Change Agile process. Don't start testing another idea until you finish one of the three.

WATCH OUT FOR THESE TRAPS!

○ Don't bitch about things that don't work without being willing to pursue making things better with your team.
○ Don't come up with solutions for things that are broken without involving your team.
○ Don't overengineer fixes to the problems you're trying to solve.

RESOURCES FOR YOU ONLINE - BESTBOSSEVER.ORG

○ One-Page Change Worksheet (for ideas going into testing)
○ Team/Department Change Worksheet (to track active ideas)
○ Graphics for Idea Evaluator, Rattle Scale, Influencer Map of Change

MORE FUN STUFF ONLINE

○ Videos on change from *Up in the Air* (George Clooney), *Apollo 13*, *Oceans 11*, and HBO's *Silicon Valley*

 KRIS DUNN

---

14. Yes, ABC actually tried a series based on the GEICO Caveman commercials in 2007. It lasted six episodes.

You Think Your Work Rival Has Declared War; She Just Thinks It's Thursday

Some people just want to watch the world burn.

Reading the corporate tea leaves is a tough assignment during times of change. Paranoia and gossip are the rules of the day.

Reading intent of others is a funny thing. You're in the workplace, and your workplace has established expectations related to change:

» We talk to each other before we make decisions or take meaningful action.

» We give people a heads up before we announce something that won't feel good to them.

» We try to play nice and, if confronted, we try to make the person confronting us feel good about our intent.

This is another way to say "there are rules." Of course, these items are norms—guidelines if you will, not hard rules. Every once in a while, you run into someone who does not give two s**ts about your norms. They do what they want, when they want, and generally don't give you the heads up that it's coming. They also won't worry about making you feel better if you ask them about it after the fact.

You know, ass####s. We're pretty quick to assign full villain status to people who don't play by the norms. Villains seem to be most active during times of high change.

What's interesting about people like this you think are enemies in the workplace is the following:

You think they're out to get you based on the chaos they cause. They probably just think it's Thursday.[1]

Translation: they generally aren't even thinking about you. Tearing s**t up is just what they do, but when they take an action that impacts us as individuals, we're likely to view the actions as a personal threat and affront. Occasionally this assessment might be true, but in my experience, people who cause chaos during times of change can be factored into three categories related to perceived slights against you:

» **They have a plan and a place they want to be unrelated to you.** They have a POA (plan of action) that's bigger than their relationship with you. You're taking it personally, but the "tearing s**t up" impacts multiple people, not just you. They're not even thinking about you. Seventy percent of the time, this is the reality.

» **They don't have a plan but love to keep everyone off balance as part of their managerial DNA.** Again, it's not about you. Their business is chaos and, by the way, the more positional power they have, the better business is—20 percent of the time, this is the reality.

» **They're out to get you.**[2] Crap, it's what you thought. They hate your guts, you're in the way and its takedown time. Ten percent of the time, this is the reality. Grab your helmet and prepare for contact.

---

1. Playlist: "Basket Case" by Green Day.
2. Or as Joseph Heller said in *Catch-22*, "Just because you're paranoid doesn't mean they aren't after you."

To determine if the frontal assault is about you or simply a broader lifestyle choice of your internal rival, just look around. If other people are irritated with the actions of your rival, it's safe to assume their actions are macro (broad preference for anarchy), not micro (seeking to destroy your career).

Unless you're experiencing flavor number three, your best strategy is to keep an eye on it but ignore it. Go about your business. You do you, let them do them, and save your emotional reaction and gun powder for when it really matters. Perhaps you could learn from the rival and start taking more proactive action in times of change as well.

If you're high sensitivity, this is going to be challenging. They're going to wear you out. You'll think it's the workplace version of Normandy.

To them, it's just Thursday. What's for lunch?

12

You're Reading Glassdoor Again?
(Talking about Compensation)

Life is a game. Money is how we keep score.
—Ted Turner

We hate talking about money with employees.

After all, if we've evolved past "do it because I said so," surely we've grown past being offended when a candidate or an employee has the audacity to ask about money, right?[1]

Without question, we should expect employees to ask questions about compensation. The problem is many of the inquiries about money are based on imperfect information and rumor, and can be asked in a vacuum without regard to performance level, career experience, and other factors that drive differences in pay.

We live in a world where companies and managers are presumed to be guilty of pay inequity.

Add that reality to the fact that most managers of people would rather lose a toe (one of the small ones, not the big one[2]) than field and close an aggressive employee question about compensation, and you've got a recipe for disaster.

The chapter title is strong to get your attention. If an employee has a point on compensation, go get help (your boss, HR, etc.) to get it fixed. Pay people what they're worth and pay the same for

---

1. Nope! "Ungrateful" and "problem child" are just a few of the unfortunate descriptors used when employees ask about money.
2. The big toe can bear twice as much weight as the other toes combined. So take the pinkie toe instead of making me answer a question about the salary you saw on Glassdoor, please.

similar experience and skills across all groups. But if an employee's compensation is appropriate for where they are in their career, you need a framework to work through the questions, take a stand, tell them no, and move forward.

Spoiler alert: It's harder than it looks. Let's get to it.

Let's Start with a Disclaimer before We Get to Business

First things first, and I'm actually saying it for the second time. Don't discriminate when it comes to pay. Got it? Great. This chapter assumes that you value people with similar knowledge, skills, abilities, and experience the same regardless of gender, race, national origin, or any other identifier, protected by law or not.

The rest of this chapter is dedicated to helping you survive questions and issues about compensation. Remember this book is for you—the manager of people—and my sole purpose is to help you get great outcomes and close business. I'm here for you, not for the haters who Monday morning quarterback every piece of advice and counsel and generally assume the worst about everyone.

The Market Never Lies and Greed Is Good

How many damn places can employees shop for salary comparisons?

Turns out, there are a LOT. In today's digital world, candidates and employees alike have never had greater access to compensation information. But the real world is more sophisticated than a Glassdoor salary estimate built on a questionable job description and limited geographic considerations, which is a fancy way of saying a lot of those sources suck.

Real talk: Your company has a position in the marketplace related to pay. It may not be the one you want, but it's all you've got.

Pay/compensation strategy (or reality, if strategy is limited) is based on the following factors for your organization:

» **Your company's maturity and financial stability.** The more mature and stable your company is, the greater its ability to pay people. Viva to long-term success when it comes to pay! Success over time yields the ability to pay.

» **Your company's philosophy on base pay (lead, match, or lag) and its level of sophistication/control related to matters of compensation.** While we all want to lead via our pay philosophy, at times that's not possible, and at times, that's not the strategy. You have to know who you are and be comfortable with that. Laggard is a tough word to hear, but it's the reality for many.

» **Your company's relative position on Total Comp versus Base Comp factors, which are generally underreported in the marketplace.** Total Comp includes factors like value of core benefits, incentive/bonus plans, and so on,[3] in addition to base earnings. Know where the value is that your company provides before you talk money with employees. Sell, baby, sell!

» **Your company's compensation plan structure.** Science! Elements include salary grades and ranges (which include a minimum, midpoint, and maximum for each job in the company) as well as comp-ratios (which help you understand at a glance an employee's position in the range). General rule of thumb: if your company doesn't have salary ranges, you're in the Wild, Wild West and money conversations are going to be harder for you to close.

---

3. "We have great benefits" is the compensation equivalent of "we have a fun culture" when you're walking a candidate through a sea of gray cubicles. Great managers get their share of talent regardless of comp strategy.

Most companies aren't out to screw employees when it comes to pay. But, make no mistake about it, your company has a different set of goals than candidates/employees when it comes to compensation.

Your company wants to set compensation at a point where it has the talent it needs to run the business, fairness and equity are present, and it can remain profitable. It doesn't want to spend more than that. That's capitalism. #freemarket

Add all of those factors up, and your company has a market position when it comes to pay.

That market position is tested every day by two things: *candidates who are thinking about joining your company* and *employees who are thinking about leaving your company.* It's a hard-knock life out there.

The market never lies. Of course, just because your company pays enough to be competitive doesn't mean your employee won't have angst about money issues.

Lucky you. Let's dig into some situations and how to deal with them.

Tool 18: How to Talk about/Frame
Compensation in the Recruiting Process
Money on The Recruiting Trail and Making Offers

Time to dance, people!

The first place you'll feel uncomfortable about money with an employee is when you're recruiting them, long before you make them an offer. The game of hide and seek is simple, as you want to know what they need to take the job you may offer, and they want to know what the job pays.[4]

---

4. Pro tip: The first person in this scenario (hiring manager or candidate) to address what everyone is thinking usually is in control and gets the best outcomes. Think of this as a first-strike advantage.

Recent changes in some state laws have made it illegal to ask a candidate what they currently make or what their compensation was in their last job. The good news is you don't have to ask them what they make/made, you simply need to understand what you can pay for the KSAs the candidate brings to the table.

The best practice is called "Compensation Framing," and it should happen as a part of your first interview with the candidate and sound like you saying something like this:

> "Sally, if you end up being the right candidate for this accounting job, the offer is likely to come in somewhere in the 55K to 62K range.
>
> "If we get to the end of the process, will that type of offer work for you?"

Boom. That's all you need to do to stop dancing. You told the candidate what the offer was going to be and asked them to tentatively confirm they could accept that offer. Film at eleven.

Here are some advanced notes on this process because I'm here for you and for the game:

» **Candidates may ask you for the salary range of the job.** Assume the full salary range of the job (minimum/maximum) is $55K to $85K, but your target hiring salary for the range is $60K, what number do you think the candidate migrates to? That's right: $85K! That's why you should proactively talk about money via the talking track provided, to eliminate doubt and misunderstandings.[5]

» **When presenting the restricted range outlined here via "framing," the top end of your range should be consistent with what you think the offer letter will say at the end of**

---

5. The normal salary range—minimum to maximum—is designed to let someone get ten to twenty years of salary increases before they hit the max. Doesn't matter, every candidate is automatically going to migrate to the max and feel cheated if you don't offer that.

the process—let's say $60K—to drive satisfaction from the candidates they got to the high end of the range. Candidates who say they'll accept the type of offer you're framing automatically go to the top of the range you provide. Shocking, I know.

» **You're asking for a commitment via this "framing" to a small range to ensure you don't waste your time with a candidate you can't afford.** My experience shows that by being direct with where the ultimate offer will come in at, everyone is happier with the process.

Treat all people fairly (across all candidates with similar skills), communicate where the offer will come in via a small range, and ask for the commitment early in the process to avoid late surprises. Being in control and closing has never been easier.

It just works. Try it.

Remind the Candidate of the Framing in the Offer Process

So you used my framing technique and got preliminary agreement from the candidate that they would accept an offer in the small, controlled range you described that was more than fair. Good job by you!

To maximize effectiveness and your close rate, you'll want to remind the candidate of their earlier agreement when you actually make them an offer at the end of the recruiting process. Something like this will suffice:

> "Sally, great news! I'm calling you today to make you an offer. If you remember, we talked about where the offer was likely to come in at ($55K to $62K), and you let me know that it would be an offer you would accept. True to my word, I'm happy to offer you the accounting position with us at $60K."

After leading with that, you can add other talking points (bonus, benefits, start date, etc.) that normally go with a verbal offer before you send your company's offer packet over. By getting agreement on an acceptable offer early in the process, you've taken guesswork out of the process and limited the amount of counteroffers from candidates you'll hear.

Pro tip: If you want to limit counters even further, provide a range up front where the top number is what you'll offer. Come in at $62K instead of $60K.[6]

You closed them on the first conversation, before most people even think about closing. Well done.

Tool 19: The Top Five Questions Employees Ask about Money
Everybody Wants Some (Questions from Employees about Money)

Of course, compensation issues/questions from candidates aren't the hard part of your job, are they?

Hells to the no. The hard questions are the ones that come from your existing employees.

Your employees are constantly bombarded with data points from the outside world that cause doubt related to their pay. The world is constantly telling them they are worth more, albeit with shaky information and comparisons that make "apples and oranges" seem like direct matches.

As a result of the world coming at them and their aspirations for more money, FUD (fear, uncertainty, and doubt) sets in. Eventually, they get their nerve up and they come to you to talk!

---

6. Double pro tip: Of course, I originally came in at $60K to reserve $2K room for negotiation for candidates who want to do that. Just saying.

You know what's coming when they set up that meeting, don't you? Here are the top questions your employees will approach you with related to money/compensation:

» "I feel like I work really hard on our team and deserve a raise for the value I add. Can I get a raise?"

» "Everyone in our department knows Riley makes more than the rest of us. That doesn't seem fair. How can I get my salary reviewed?"

» "My friend at Theranos works in a similar position and makes $80,000. Why don't I make that much? Can I get a raise?"[7]

» "Glassdoor shows that most companies pay people in my position more than I'm currently making. Why don't I make that much?"

» "I get calls from recruiters, and if I can't get a raise, I'll probably start looking. Can you help me?"[8]

Daaaaaamn. You would have faked a cell phone call had you known this was coming. Who among us hasn't felt the pressure of the seemingly unanswerable question about money?

The Worst Thing You Can Do Is Not Close Out Comp Questions or Blame Someone Else

I know what you're thinking. You didn't sign up for this s**t. Hell, you'd like more money too, but are you complaining? No!

Check your ego at the door. If you're going to be a manager of choice at your company, you'll need to own the response to these questions.

---

7. And then I said, "Didn't I just read that Theranos is pretty much out of business and the founder is going to prison?"
8. Don't be afraid to ask them for details about the calls from recruiters. It's part of the Career Agent vibe/role.

If your company has any type of comp ranges in place, is generally in line with the market, and applies compensation consistently across employees with the same KSAs, odds are that the answer is "no" 85 to 90 percent of the time when employees ask for more money or a raise.

Note that this doesn't mean you're telling the employee that the pay at your company is as high as they can get elsewhere. Your job is not to match compensation anywhere in America, it's to make sure people are paid fairly and consistently within your organization.

"I feel good about where you're at related to pay."[9]

—A seasoned manager who knows she has to shut a comp question down or it will haunt her forever

How do you get into a conversation about comp with a direct report and close the issue down?

I thought you'd never ask.

Tool 20: The Acknowledge/Engage/Close Method for Compensation Questions from Employees
How to Answer Compensation Questions from Employees: A Framework

Like any other important conversation you have with one of your team members, you want to be prepared. That's why I've created this handy, easy-to-use framework for any compensation conversation you have with a direct report on your team called *Acknowledge/Engage/Close*.

I know. Sounds clinical as hell, right? As you'll find out, it's up to you to make it sound conversational and feel like it's coming from

---

9. The most powerful thing a manager can say related to compensation, but it scares the hell out of most managers.

you. But it works well to guide, explore, and close out any question about compensation coming from a member of your team.

Here are the highlights of the framework with some sample phraseology to use in your response to close out the question:

» **Acknowledge:** Dr. Phil time. Field the question from your employee with empathy, noting you understand the question and reinforce that the question is important to you. Translation: Don't be a jerk; instead, make them feel like it's important to you, which it should be. Take your ego out of it.

Examples of "Acknowledge" key phrases:

> "I understand what you're asking."
> "Let's get that question answered."
> "You're super important to the team."
> "I always want you to be paid fairly."

» **Engage:** Provide a broad overview of your company's approach to compensation, highlighting the fact that your company is dedicated to ensuring compensation is competitive.[10] Some of you are skeptical as you read this. What's the alternative? Tell your employee the company doesn't care? You simply have to tell them—in a way that matches the approach as you understand it—that your company looks to the market when it decides what to pay people.

Examples of "Engage" key phrases:

> "We have a process to determine what competitive compensation is."

---

10. You'll need some help from your HR team with this. Go get this info before you hear comp questions.

> › "We use external data sources to benchmark compensation data and ensure we are competitive."
> › "We use that data to bring people into the company in a fair, equitable, and competitive way based on their roles."
> › "We use career bands and salary ranges to track process and maintain competitiveness."

» **Close:** Ah, the hard part! Let them know that you believe their compensation is in line with the outside world for their job in your organization (note, if you are unsure, you can go away and do the research and come back to this step). After providing your analysis, remind them of any opportunities that exist for them to increase their compensation (annual increases, promotional opportunities, etc.). Don't forget to close upbeat. If you're happy that they're part of the team, tell them that!

Examples of "Close" key phrases:

> › "I feel good about where you are at."
> › "We use annual performance check-ins to review and make adjustments as needed."
> › "I appreciate you being comfortable enough to ask me about this."
> › "You're important to the team and our company."
> › "I'm always open to talking about things that are important to you."

For best results, memorize the words that make up this framework—Acknowledge/Engage/Close—then remember the one to two key phrases in each step.

Don't be stressed—if you hit each of the three steps in some fashion and deliver it in a manner that sounds like you, you'll be in the top 10 percent of all managers who respond to compensation questions from their employees.

There Are Only Three Scenarios When
Employees Ask Money-Related Questions

So now you've got the tool to respond to any comp question you'll hear in your life as a manager. But the path varies a bit based on the situation at hand when an individual asks for more money. Here's your map and how to use the tool depending on the circumstances:

» **The employee's comp is fine.** You know it before they even finish the question.[11] You need to tell them that. Proceed with the entire mapped talking points appropriate for the employee—Acknowledge/Engage/Close—when you hear the question. If they're where they need to be and you know it, there's no reason to delay. Work through the entire tool. Close this thing out.

» **You're not sure their compensation is where it needs to be.** You've got some work to do. Hit the "Acknowledge" talking track, then let them know you need a few days to research it and come back to them. Find that help from HR and your boss, then set up dedicated time to come back to them and work through the entire Acknowledge/Engage/Close framework. If a change is needed, add that to your talking points. If no adjustment is being made, tell them that and include the research you did in the "Engage" section before you close it out in "Close."

» **You 100 percent know that their compensation is below where it needs to be.** See the "Acknowledge" track. Acknowledge, tell them you need to research, go find help, and set up a time to follow up. Once you are in the follow-up session, work through all the steps of the tool within the "Engage" section detailing what you found, the adjustment you're prepared to make, and some confident remarks about effectively

---

11. You may have an out-of-body experience as your worst performer is asking for more money. Deep breaths.

addressing the gap. Close upbeat and tell them how much you value them.

Note that if you're not comfortable saying "no" to a request for more money in the same conversation your employee asks the question, the second scenario here is always your play. That gives you more time to review the conversation you need to have and deliver on the Acknowledge/Engage/Close tool.

Don't hide from conversations about money. Embrace them for the opportunities they are to be transparent and honest with your team.

And, of course, always be closing.

Be Proactive, My Friends

You can't stop questions about money, but you can take a proactive approach to compensation. As you build your team, add new hires, make promotions, and so on, small issues can crop up. Differences between people in the same job title can be created, and compression between team members at different levels can occur.

The evolved manager looks at the compensation of this team, with titles, time in role, and other factors at least three to four times a year. Run a report and look at it. Are you proud of the links between KSAs, performance, and career level?[12] Can you defend it? Are you at risk of losing someone due to a blind spot?

Never wait for trouble. If you see an issue on your team, get it fixed before they ask.

An ounce of prevention is worth a pound of cure. Benjamin Franklin can't be wrong.

---

12. Avoid being tricked by recency bias, good or bad. Think about the entire last year when comparing employees and compensation levels.

KD'S CHEAT SHEET: CONVERSATIONS ABOUT COMPENSATION / MONEY WITH EMPLOYEES

DO THIS!

- Be proactive in pitching what an offer is likely to look like in your first conversation with employees.
- Remind candidates at the point of offer of their tentative agreement to an acceptable offer earlier in the process.
- Know the major types of compensation questions/challenges likely to come your way from existing employees.
- Memorize the simple Acknowledge/Engage/Close framework and be ready to use it in compensation conversations with employees.
- Understand the scenarios (compensation is OK, you're not sure, or needs fixing) and use the Acknowledge/Engage/Close framework appropriately.

WATCH OUT FOR THESE TRAPS!

- Don't wait for a candidate to ask you about money before addressing it as a hiring manager.
- Don't be stressed by money questions for existing employees; they are a normal and healthy part of your life as a manager of people.
- Don't leave questions about money hanging for more than a couple of days; close them out.
- Don't push blame to the company's approach on compensation, even if deserved. You have to own issues on money with your team.
- Don't be defensive as soon as you hear issues about money.

RESOURCES FOR YOU ONLINE - BESTBOSSEVER.COM

- A deeper dive on the Acknowledge/Engage/Close framework with extended talking tracks for your use
- Extended descriptions of goals, objectives, and common components of Formal Compensation Plans in corporate America
- An extended case study on the use of "framing" with candidates as part of the recruiting process

MORE FUN STUFF ONLINE

- Video clips, including John Travolta getting a raise from his manager in *Saturday Night Fever* and his dad not being impressed, as well as Jonah Hill asking Leonardo DiCaprio to prove how much he makes a month in *Wolf of Wall Street*

 KRIS DUNN

Bonus

What Type of Offer Does It Take to Get a Great Candidate to Switch Companies

I'm writing this book in 2022, basically two years after the start of the pandemic and in one of the hardest labor/talent crunches we've seen in our lifetimes.

There's no reason to assume it's going to get easier to hire in the next decade. Direct applicants for open jobs at your career site are also significantly down, which points to a sobering reality:

The days of posting a job and simply hiring someone who applies are ending.[1] You're going to have to go out, find passive candidates who are already employed, and give them great reasons to consider joining your team.

Hiring is getting harder, and you're going to have to go steal someone else's talent more than you have in the past. Lucky you!

The best reason a candidate has to accept a job offer from you is your reputation as someone who grows people's careers. Be "awesome to work for," please.

But even if you're the personification of a Career Agent, money is *always* part of the equation, which begs a question for you to consider: What type of money offer does it take to get a great candidate to switch companies? Note that "switch" indicates the candidate is currently employed, and let's assume they're currently holding the same kind of job as the one you currently have open.

---

1. This is called "post and pray" in the recruiting game. Answered prayers related to candidates are trending way down.

My experience says that the happiness and security of a candidate at their current company drives what it will take from a monetary perspective to get them to leave. The "happiness/how much is it going to take" continuum works like this.

» **The chronically unhappy or those in danger of losing their job will leave for a lateral pay move or a very small bump in compensation.** All you have to do is ask nicely! This includes candidates inside struggling companies that are experiencing layoffs, as well as those who are in stable organizations but working for a manager whom they can't stand, or those who have low satisfaction with their current role. You'll hear the fear or loathing in their voice at times if you listen closely, which should make you ponder whether they'll be happy with you.[2]

» **Candidates who are at least somewhat content with their organization, job, and manager will still listen to recruiters.** But it will take a better offer to get them to make a move, because there is always risk in making a change. The bidding for this group starts with the equivalent of a promotional pay bump, which is in the 8 to 15 percent range. They're saying "while I like it here, I don't love it here." This group is gettable and a lot of you can afford to pay the ransom in question.[3]

» **Back up the Brinks truck for candidates who are happy, engaged, and working for someone they respect and admire.** They're still willing to listen, but like the Godfather, you'll have to make them an offer they can't refuse—a 16 to 30 percent bump in pay is likely to get their attention. But beware! This group is most susceptible to counteroffers due to their satisfaction level and positive relationships inside their current company. You're also going to destroy your internal

---

2. You're awesome, of course. But are they awesome? It's a fair question when you hear even moderate trash talking.
3. A big part of whether this group switches is your connection with the candidate. Smiles everyone! Let's sell!

equity unless you run across someone severely undervalued in the marketplace.

While total compensation related to benefits, bonus, and other items is important, candidates are always going to initially evaluate other opportunities via the base salary or hourly rate in question. Straight cash, homie.[4]

In tight labor markets, smart leaders get creative related to getting the talent they need, especially if they're constrained from a compensation perspective. Two plays to get the talent you need if you can't offer 20 percent increases to external candidates include the following:

» **Get busy locating internal employees who can be developed and promoted.** Sounds simple, but most of you are so busy you don't make the time investment to think about what's possible with internal candidates. Developing your own succession plan using employees at lower or lateral levels is smart. Engaging those individuals with meaningful project work and other items of influence before you need them in the next role is brilliant.

» **Be open to external candidates at the next level down from the position you have open.** Hire the person, not the résumé. If you're hiring a manager of accounting, it's relatively easy to find ten external candidates who are accountants who would love the opportunity. In that group of ten, there's likely one candidate who rises above the rest and is "ready now," but you'll never know that unless you do the work and dig in. You get bonus points if you're networking externally to identify some of these recruits before you have the need.

---

4. Randy Moss's 2005 answer to reporters when questioned on how he paid an NFL fine for an obscene gesture in a game.

Careers are ladders. The better you sell the job, yourself as a manager, and the company, the more you'll get talented candidates to make the switch.

Many of you are going to chase candidates you can't afford. That's a trap you should avoid.

To make sure you're managing your own expectations on the "recruitability" of external candidates, consider hiring probability. Hiring probability is defined as the level of certainty that you will get an accepted offer from the candidate, and they'll start work for your company.

Hiring probability is a swag percentage estimate that keeps it real when chasing talent. You can throw out a hiring probability number when you see a résumé for the first time, when you have a signed offer, and everything in between. Is it 10, 45, or 95 percent? How confident are you that you can get them to join your company and team?

The percentage goes up and down depending on the aforementioned factors—expected compensation, perceived satisfaction with current job, manager, and company, and a hundred other issues you feel in your gut.

Swag a percentile for hiring probability on the candidate you love. Are you in the game or chasing talent that's going to crush you at the end?[5]

Compensation is a marketplace. Maximizing the talent on your team requires you to be a trader and understand who's gettable and who's not when hiring for your team.

---

5. Be honest. If you say 70 percent, it's more like 50/50 once you take your rose-colored glasses off.

13

I'm Thrilled to Announce You Met Expectations This Year

(Performance Management)

Everyone has a photographic memory;
some just don't have film.
—Steven Wright

The Moment You Love to Hate

No one likes to do performance reviews as a manager. If you do, you probably enjoy light-to-moderate forms of pain, books about war, and have a lifetime license to Microsoft Project.[1]

The issue, of course, is surprise. It's cliché to say, but performance reviews should never be a bombshell. If you've got your eye on the Best Boss Ever Formula, you've engaged in a steady stream of goals and feedback throughout the year, delivered with empathy and a career-building focus.

But you have to do the work all year long to make formal performance feedback (and yes, performance reviews) a nonevent. Because if you don't do the work, the following events in front of you to complete the performance cycle are going to suck:

---

1. No, you can't buy a lifetime MS Project license, and the fact you inquired says everything I needed to know but was afraid to ask. You'll have to subscribe to Office 365 like everyone else.

» **Trying to determine ratings for your direct report** (we'd all love a world where you could simply go "thumbs up/thumbs down," but it's always more complicated than that).

» **Writing the actual performance review** (you're no Malcolm Gladwell, my friend).

» **Sitting down with your direct report and attempting not to be a complete ****ing robot** (Steve, thanks for joining me today . . . <barf>).

» **Asking them to sign a performance review** (look at you—a junior lawyer, just like your mom wanted you to be).

When you do the work throughout the year, these things are easy. When you don't do the work, the night (also known as the performance review session) is dark and full of terrors, similar to the events in the movie franchise *The Purge*.

Bell Curves, Forced Rankings, and Your Softness

First things first, I'm a realist. You should be one as well.

Not everyone on your team is a star. Some of you reading this book long to please others, while some just give in to the fact that it's easier to tell people what they want to hear when giving up a top rating. Both factors can seep into your life as a manager of people.

You should think about the performance of your team like a bell curve—a normal distribution of reality and outcomes. If you have a team of two, it's possible that you have two stars. If you have a team of four or more people, I'm here with the unfortunate news that I smell BS when you tell me they all are crushing it.[2]

I'll spare you the sermon about the bell curve other than to say for every ten people in corporate America, only two or three of the ten are stars. Most of the rest are doing fine, but they aren't the

---

2. So much so that I automatically assign you to the left of the bell curve of managers when you rate all six of your direct reports as "exceeds."

Steph Curry of their domain. Your job is to provide real feedback and measurement and migrate them *toward* being stars.

The naysayers of understanding performance distribution will try and shame you,[3] claiming that you're doing a forced ranking process of your people, aka Jack Welch in the glory days of General Electric.

Pay them no mind. We're not doing forced ranking here. We're simply remembering that calling someone a "top performer" is something that's earned and should never be taken lightly.

Measuring Performance Is Linked to Earlier Themes of Goal Setting and Coaching

If you wait until HR sends you a message with a deadline for annual review submittals, you're screwed. Simply put, if you're looking for a performance review to be a nonevent, you have to put in the work on the following items months (if not a full year) in advance:

» **Did you set good goals the employee could be measured on?** We covered the smorgasbord of goal types early, but don't be a pig. The right goals, rather than a bunch of goals, are the key.

» **Metrics.** You love them. But simply picking goal types that provide clean metrics is a trap. You'll likely need a mix of goals with clear metrics and ones that require you to observe, think for yourself, and provide feedback that you'll have to own with your employee.

» **Manager observation.** Speaking of thinking for yourself, you can have a slate of goals that's 100 percent based on your observations rather than numbers. You just have to get comfortable

---

3. The same people might tell you that merit and high performance don't exist. Okay, Comrades!

identifying whether someone is good or great at the area in question, which we'll talk about at length coming up.

» **Coaching along the way.** If you're not using the coaching tool we covered earlier at least a couple of times a week, I've got a nickname for you: *Dr. Feelgood.*[4] Most of your employees aren't stars, but because you won't coach on a regular basis, they probably think they are.

When it comes to performance management, performance reviews, and rating your direct reports, you either did the work (throughout the year) or you didn't.

Types of Performance Reviews

There are really three types of performance review formats that exist in global corporations. Check it out:

» **The Generic** ("Performance Reviews for Dummies"). In this review, the company has prepopulated ten to twenty things for you to review your employees on, mostly driven by dimensions like "teamwork" and "initiative." The form is the same for all positions, whether you're an engineer or a janitor. Enjoy the blandness of this unsalted cracker of corporate life.[5]

» **The Custom** ("Trigonometry for Managers"). The exact opposite of the generic, this review system provides a shell format, and asks you (the managers) to insert all goals the employee is chasing in a given year. It's a powerful format but, like an AR-15, is dangerous in the wrong hands.

---

4. If rat-tailed Jimmy is on your team, note that he's a secondhand hood and deals out of Hollywood. The Crue fans understand what I'm saying.
5. The equivalent of dumbing down performance to a paint-by-numbers coloring book. Hope you can handle that.

» **The Two-Section Hybrid** ("The Smooth Blend"). The preferred format of your humble author, this review format blends the previous two, with Section One providing a shell format for the manager to insert meaningful goals customized for the position, and Section Two being predetermined competencies, values, or potential factors that require less prework on your behalf. At its best, this hybrid format becomes the basis for measuring performance in the job (Section One) versus potential (Section Two).

The keys to the performance review game are simple. The more the review format provides open space to be defined by you (the manager), the more you need to make smart decisions early and migrate to goal sets like the Big Five (discussed earlier) that can plug into that space.

Once that's done, your daily/weekly on-the-fly coaching should contrast good versus great performance in those areas.

Tool 21: How to Collect Performance Info throughout the Year

Let's say you've got your arms around everything we've covered to this point. Now you're sitting at your laptop ready to pull it all together, rate someone's performance, and actually write a performance review. The cursor is blinking in front of you.

Awkward.

There's just one problem. You've got memory issues that rival Jason Bourne trying to remember what the hell happened at Project Treadstone.

A lot of s**t goes down performance-wise during the course of a year. If you try and remember it all, you'll fail and be subject to a variety of biases, most notably the power of the "recency bias" (the things you remember from the recent past get more weight than they should) and the "like-me" bias (you're just naturally drawn to your mini-me's—you know, the ones wearing Lululemon gear).

Simply put, you need to collect performance feedback throughout the year to make sure you have the data/info you need. Some of you work at companies where you can put performance notes in a performance management system, etc. If that works for you, do it.

But most of us live our lives in email as leaders, which means email is your best bet to collect performance snippets in a fluid way throughout the year. For best results, do the following:

1. **Create a master email folder for performance feedback** for your entire team, then create subfolders for each team member.[6]
2. **As good or bad feedback on a direct report comes in via email, simply drag that info into the direct report's folder.** Don't worry about saving too much to each folder; it's better to have too much at the end of a review period than to have too little.
3. **As you make random observations about performance that are notable, send yourself an email with a note on what you observed about an employee** (good or bad), and whenever you get around to it, flow it into the direct report's folder. Sending yourself a performance note via email is key to capturing meaningful nuggets when mobile in meetings, away from your desk, or thinking wistfully in traffic about why Bob keeps screwing up your pet project.

That's right. I'm telling you more email, not less, is the answer. The world wants you to believe that email is the devil, and in some cases that's true. But the world isn't responsible for remembering how Bethany rocked the marketing automation launch or how

---

6. To reinforce use of these folders, you could use nicknames that make you smile every time you drop a feedback note in these systems. Be kind with the nicknames and assume an employee will see them someday.

Patrick talked about his personal life multiple times and made a key client feel gross.[7]

Email folders are your hack to never forget the good and the bad that happened in March when you're staring at a blank review in December.

Tool 22: How to Determine the Right Performance Rating in Any Area

When you're trying to review an employee, you've got things you need to rate them on, and you've got "stuff" in each area to consider.[8]

But how do you get to the actual rating? Try this simple flow:

Observations = Trend = Reality = Rating

When you're trying to rate an employee in any area and you're either struggling or need to check yourself, the chain of evidence works as follows:

1. **You start with the performance data you've collected, which are *observations*.** If you've got metrics, those are considered here as well. Don't forget that your own manager observations (and those of others) collected throughout the year should also weigh heavily into the collective vibe.
2. **Those observations start to form *trends*.** Trends show you may have something that you can base a rating on.
3. **See a trend consistently enough over a period of time, and that trend becomes a *reality*.** That reality means you've got what you need to rate someone's performance in the area in question.

---

7. And don't tell me about your stellar use of Slack or similar chat tool. The fact you'll email me about it proves my point. Email is king.
8. Highly technical term. But let's face it, this is more art than science.

4. **Since you've now got a reality set in your mind related to the employee's performance level, the only question left is what *rating* to give.** Get your mind around thresholds that you'll set for each rating point in your company's rating scale. Then, think about where the performance reality falls in those anchors and assign a rating.

When in doubt, go with your gut related to the rating. But if you use the formula—Observations = Trend = Reality = Rating—and consider data and observation from the entire rating period, you'll have done more than enough to overcome any of the common biases that prevent you from accurately rating someone's performance.

The Thin Red Line of Rating Scales and Bailing Out as a Manager

Let's talk about where you're going to bail out and show weakness as a manager, otherwise known as your company's rating scale.

There are two primary forms of rating scales in the performance review world. The five-point scale or the three-point scale, constructed something like this:

» **Five-Point Performance Rating Scale**

5 = Exceeds

4 = Above Average

3 = Meets

2 = Below Average

1 = Does Not Meet

» **Three-Point Performance Rating Scale**

2 = Exceeds

1 = Meets

0 = Does Not Meet

I know what you're thinking. You're saying to yourself, "Thanks for the deep info, KD," and otherwise mocking me for the basic outline of how performance review ratings work.

But I list the scales to help illustrate where 80 percent of you will give up/give in when reviewing performance. Left unchecked, many of you will look at the hard conversation to be had during a performance review and say, "Nah, we're good," opting out of real feedback via one of two of the following classic sell-outs when reviewing performance:

» **The Five-Point Scale Sell-Out:** You have ten things to rate a direct employee on. They're doing fine but not really excelling at anything. The right rating on all items is a "3" or "meets" expectations. But you really don't want to face a conversation that tells them they're average, so out of the ten items to be rated, you mix in three ratings of "4" or "above average." The result? An overall average rating of 3.3. You look at that and are still uncomfortable, so you change one more item rating to a "4" to get to an overall rating of 3.4.[9]

   Look at my smart friend manipulate the system! You put the 3.4 in front of the employee and they round it up and think to themselves, "Kris thinks I'm better than average, maybe even a star" and decide to let you off the hook in the performance review session and challenge nothing. The session goes smoothly with no meaningful conversation. You've lost all leverage to get more out of the direct report by caving when it came time to discuss merely good versus great. Congrats!

» **The Three-Point Scale Sell-Out:** Sneaky HR types (like me) see you caving in the manner described here and decide to move to the three-point scale, taking the "above average" rating

---

9. This happens so much that Moderna should create a vaccine to protect managers from the virus, and we should do a vaccine mandate for this under OSHA rules. Note: I own Moderna stock.

away. You respond by saying, "hold my beer" and do the ultimate sell out, giving the same employee a rating of "exceeds"
instead of "meets" to get similar sell-out math.

It's called rating inflation, my friends. Sometimes you don't
even know you're doing it, but your mind is fleeing subconsciously
from perceived conflict.

Of course, the sell-outs described are why some companies insti-
tute a form of forced distribution, dictating only a specific percentage of overall performance reviews can rise to the highest rating.
Turns out we're to blame when companies do forced rankings.
Good times.

The Real Difference in Meets versus Exceeds

Some of you read the sell-out descriptions in the previous section
and became defensive.

"Melinda really deserved the Exceeds ratings I gave her, KD."

Did she? Are you sure?

What should be the driving force between giving someone an
"exceeds" rating over a "meets" rating on any performance goal?

»   One word: "*Innovate*"
»   Two words: "*Innovate and Create*"

Simply put, you should reserve the rare air of the "exceeds
rating" for those who create value beyond what's expected in their
job. It's not enough for someone to simply make more widgets,
answer more calls, or give more of whatever production measurement you use to truly differentiate themselves from the pack.

If you're in the middle ground trying to determine whether
someone deserves the highest rating, think about the following
adjective sets:

» **Examples of Identifiers Signaling "Meets" Behavior (Expectations!):** Quality, Quantity, Accuracy, Timeliness, Respect for Others, Integrity, Communicates Effectively, Accountable, Pride-in-Work Product, Team Player.

» **Examples of Identifiers Signaling "Exceeds" Behavior (Differentiators!):** Proactive, Creative, Innovative, Leads By Example, Seeks Greater Responsibility, Self-Motivated, Solution-Oriented, Always Learning, Takes Chances, Builds Teams.[10]

That's a pretty good list. Apply these identifiers across any functional area to identify the true players—the ones who will not only help you maintain the status quo, but will blow up the status quo as necessary. When you find them, reward them, and guard against rating inflation in your organization—lest you drive the true performers away because they feel like you'll give anyone an "exceeds."

Tool 23: How to Write Performance Reviews That Don't Suck

Of course, at some point, you're going to have to write a summary that will support the rating you gave a direct report in any area. I call these review "items," and they're the bane of most managers' existence when it comes to rating performance. After all, you didn't sign up for the job to be a writer, and most of you don't have a degree in English or creative writing.[11]

Good news: I've got the format to ease your pain. Here's your breakdown to write great performance review items in the shortest time possible:

---

10. Most of these can be summarized by the phrase "Discretionary Effort." If someone goes beyond what's asked for on a routine basis and performance checks out otherwise, they're probably eligible for the highest rating.
11. Shout out to my Liberal Arts grads kicking a** and taking names in corporate America. Send me a haiku with feedback on the book.

[<Statement +2> + <+1 Stretch> = Gold] =
Great Performance Review Writing

Let's break this tool down:

» **Starting with <Statement +2>:** Once you've arrived at a
rating, you're going to make a statement that describes why
you're giving the rating in question. Then, you're going to back
up the statement/rating with two specific performance/behav-
ioral examples that you can cite from the review period. The specific examples you give should be representative of the trend you
see and should help you illustrate why someone is at the rating
you're giving and not the next highest point on the rating scale.
Unless your employee is getting a horrible review, you should
write these with a positive vibe. After all, there's nothing wrong
with meeting expectations—celebrate it in your writing style.

» **Adding a <+1 Stretch>:** Once you've made your statement
capturing why you rated the employee as you did in the area
in question and added two examples to back it up, it's time to
add a stretch goal that positions you as a coach. What can the
employee do in the coming months to raise their performance
in the area in question to the next available rating? This is where
you tell them what they have to do to improve the rating.

The [<Statement +2> + <1 Stretch> = Gold] tool is designed to
take generalities out of the performance review equation. You still
make your general statement, but you back it up with two examples
that are representative of clear trends you've seen in your data collection, then end with at least one specific thing they can do to move
their performance in question to the next level.

It's a simple, but amazingly effective approach to writing performance review items. It's also going to set you up to be a performance coach when you're ready to deliver the performance review
live with your direct report.

You need an example, right?

No problem. Let's do an illustration of my writing-item formula in action. Here's an item based on a financial analyst performance goal of delivering monthly forecasts in a timely and accurate fashion (meets performance):

> Eric's done a solid job at creating and executing a monthly forecast process for the company that's sustainable moving forward. He's developed relationships with all the department leaders to get the information he needs (great examples: working hard with difficult clients in the Marketing and Engineering groups) and trained them as needed (see the training he developed and rolled out across all managers at our location). He's also trained himself on the sales process for our company so he better understands how our revenue projections work.
>
> To get to the next level, I'd like to see Eric become more comfortable in challenging revenue assumptions that are being made by our divisional leaders so we have a higher degree of forecast accuracy on a monthly basis.

Got it? Not quite? Let's break that statement down related to the [<Statement +2> + <1 Stretch> = Gold] tool:

> **STATEMENT:** Eric's done a solid job at creating and executing a monthly forecast process for the company that's sustainable moving forward.
>
> **+2:** He's developed relationships with all the department leaders to get the information he needs (great examples: working hard with difficult clients in the Marketing and Engineering groups) and trained them as needed (see the training he developed and rolled out across all managers at our location). He's also trained himself on the sales

process for our company so he better understands how our revenue projections work.

+1 STRETCH: To get to the next level, I'd like to see Eric become more comfortable in challenging revenue assumptions that are being made by our divisional leaders so we have a higher degree of forecast accuracy on a monthly basis.

That's all you have to do. Do it for every performance review item you have to write, and you'll never be looking for things to say or how to say them.

Go Develop Your Own Culture of Performance as a Manager of People

Providing performance feedback and doing performance reviews is a universally loathed activity in the business world, but it doesn't have to be that way.

Set the right goals, coach daily, contrast good versus great on a regular basis, and you'll be shocked by the following outcome:

> Employees who are provided great performance feedback and rated as "meets" are often happier than those at the same performance level rated at "exceeds."

How can this be? It all comes down to your investment of time in feedback and in delivering that feedback in a way that makes the employee believe you're doing everything in your power to make them as good as they can be.

Employees with managers who are Career Agents believe in the future.

Be a Career Agent, and also be looking to migrate your employee to "great" status, even when the conversation is uncomfortable.

KD'S CHEAT SHEET: PERFORMANCE MANAGEMENT AND REVIEWS

DO THIS!

- Get mentally prepared that part of your job is to separate good versus great performance.
- Set up systems in the tools you use (hello, email!) to capture performance feedback from others on the fly.
- Add your own performance notes and observations to the systems you have set up on a weekly basis for every employee.
- Use the tools provided in this chapter to write effective "items" or backup language in your performance review to justify the rating in question.

WATCH OUT FOR THESE TRAPS!

- Don't bail the employee out by rating them higher than their actual performance dictates.
- Don't reward more base production with an "exceeds" rating unless you're getting discretionary effort that innovates or goes the extra mile.
- Don't overweight recent events/performance, whether good or bad.

RESOURCES FOR YOU ONLINE - BESTBOSSEVER.ORG

- Additional examples of performance review "item writing," including writing examples for company values, competencies, and/or potential factors

MORE FUN STUFF ONLINE

- Live performance review clips from *Scrubs* (Dr. Cox reviews J.D.) and *The Colbert Report*

 KRIS DUNN

Part III

Other Stuff We Should Talk About

14

If I'm Here and You're Here, Doesn't That Make It Our Time?
(One-on-One Meetings)

The person who knows HOW will always have a job.
The person who knows WHY will always be his boss.
—Alanis Morissette

So you've hired well, set goals, coached your butt off, and otherwise just overachieved as a manager, serving as a beacon of hope in your grasp of the core skills needed to become someone's *Best Boss Ever.* Nice!

But if you're managing white-collar, professional-grade positions at any career level, the world is going to tell you that there's another best practice that is nonnegotiable:

The recurring one-on-one meeting with each of your direct reports.[1]

I'm not here to tell you that having recurring one-on-ones (from this point forward shown as 1:1s) is wrong. The concept is full of good intent and can be value-added.

But the reality of 1:1s is they have to be executed a specific way, or your employees will think the whole idea sucks every time they

---

1. The dirty secret related to 1:1s is that both managers and employees too often exhale in disappointment whenever they check their calendar and see a 1:1 coming up in the next two hours.

see a calendar notification reminding them it's time to slog over to your office or Zoom/MS Teams event.

It's on you to suck less when it comes to 1:1s.

Let's Start with a Simple Definition

When it comes to 1:1s, your goals should be to (1) not be lame, and (2) provide a safe space where direct reports can and will talk about anything they're experiencing in their role on your team (think "circle of trust" or some other warmth-providing term).

You want a definition? *A 1:1 is a regular check-in between a direct report and a manager.* It's used to give feedback, keep each other in the loop, resolve issues, and help the participants grow in their roles. 1:1s happen in a recurring fashion on calendars, with the most popular frequency being weekly (real talk: most of us can't live up to weekly).

To the micromanagers of the world: *1:1s are not the time to methodically work through status updates of the employee's entire universe of goals, projects, and responsibilities.* That's cringe behavior, and some of you have learned this method from people you've worked for in the past.

Renounce these past ways quicker than Eddie Murphy jokes from 1987 (HBO special *Raw*) and come to the light, my students.

Do You Really Need an Hour Every Week?
On Frequency and Length of 1:1s

The first decision you have to make regarding 1:1s is how often to put them on the calendar. As it turns out, this is a tricky initial decision. Work through your decision tree with the following in mind:

»   **The world will tell you that weekly 1:1s with direct reports are the de facto standard.** You should challenge this conventional wisdom immediately. Still, you're going to have to make a decision and send the life-giving "recurring meeting request" related to your 1:1.[2]

» **Alternatives are available.** If weekly feels like too much (and it should), it's notable that monthly isn't often enough, and every two weeks is a play that feels weird unless you match it up with your company's pay dates and start each 1:1 by exclaiming "It's payday ******!" (insert language to match your brand).

» **Don't forget you can agree to skip 1:1s.** The professional play is probably to give in to the world's expectation and book weekly, with the caveat that if you and your direct report feel synched up in a given week, you'll just message each other and agree that "we're good" and skip 1:1s as necessary. Be careful not to make this the standard, however, lest it seem like you don't care about your employee.

Length of 1:1s follows the same vibe. The world expects hour-long blocks, and you'll be tempted to book thirty minutes. Do what the world expects (book an hour) with the agreement with your direct report that you'll be happy to break early anytime you can.

Career Agents Let Their People Lead

One-on-ones are the human growth hormone of leading teams, minus the back acne and other pesky physical ramifications. Any 1:1 is focused on giving the employee what they need to be successful. To really hit that goal, you're going to have to let your employees lead, which looks like this in practice:

---

2. Basic human reactions to frequency of Outlook recurring meetings: weekly (hate and rage), biweekly (acceptance and gratitude), and monthly (forgotten until fifteen minutes before the meeting).

» **Set the expectation that your direct report is going to lead the 1:1.** To take the aforementioned wisdom of Jeff Spicoli a step further: it's not "our time," it's actually "your time" (the direct report). This mindset requires some specific communication to get your people into the flow. More on how to frame this in a bit.

» **Require your employees to come with a list of things they'd like to discuss.** Your direct reports exist somewhere in the Nine-Box Grid of life. Some will naturally come with a list, many won't. So you'll need to tell them to come with a list. Do they need to share it with you beforehand? That's a style/brand question to you. The upside of sharing it before is your ability to prep, but who are we kidding? You'll have limited time to prep. A better approach might be to tell them just to bring the list with them, and you'll react and engage like you're doing an "ask me anything" AMA session on a fringe Reddit channel.

» **Lean into the awkwardness of this approach like you do a romantic scene from a John Hughes movie.** The Naturals will do what you expect them to do—crush it. Others will struggle because they've never been in charge. At times, it's going to be as awkward as Cameron in *Ferris Bueller's Day Off.*[3] Don't bail them out, because the process is part of the growth cycle. After six 1:1s, they'll pick up the flow, and you'll be as proud of them as Ferris was when Cameron decided to tell his dad that he ran up the miles of the Ferrari on a school-skipping Chicago bender.

Things to Talk About in 1:1s

The best 1:1s (the kind where the direct report gets the most value) are free-ranging conversations, which is a fancy way of saying you can talk about anything. If you're going to be the coach you know

---

3. Ferris Bueller on Cameron (which applies to your conversationally awkward employees): "Pardon my French, but Cameron is so tight that if you stuck a lump of coal up his a**, in two weeks you'd have a diamond."

you can be, you'll have to be comfortable with a wide range of topics in 1:1s, including the following:

» **Where the employee is stuck.** This should be the hottest topic in your 1:1s. It's not about you getting an update on goals and deliverables, it's about your direct report feeling comfortable enough to tell you what's broken so they can get help. When you hear the struggle, remember the 1:1 is a safe place. Your job is to help, not note struggles for use in a performance improvement plan at a later date.

» **What they don't know how to do.** This one takes a more active ear, as you'll hear your employee describe action plans that are incorrect or omit something key. Pro tip: Coach from the lens of how you learned the skill or concept in question, including failures early in your career. Bonding 101. "Everyone join hands" vibe activated.

» **Tools they need and don't have.** Do they really need the tools or is there a workaround? Your experience probably suggests that there's a way, and you should share the expectation that they can still get the task/project done and brainstorm with them about the best way to handle it in an imperfect world.

» **People who are blocking them and must be dealt with.** Here we go! The good stuff! There are always evildoers out there blocking your people from getting things done, and your direct reports at times will be paralyzed related to how to deal with the internal politics. Your job is to grow your team members in this area, teaching them the way of *The Prince* (Niccolò Machiavelli) and *The Art of War* (Sun Tzu) without completely disparaging company employees outside your team and making it "us versus them."[4] This one is a tightrope, but your employee needs you, so go there you must.

---

4. I wouldn't recommend using actual Machiavelli or Sun Tzu quotes as part of your game. There's something off-putting about laying out a "It is double pleasure to deceive the deceiver" quote when troubleshooting a project with your peeps.

» **Teammates who are less than optimized.** Sometimes the blockers aren't in other departments, they're on your team. You'll have to embrace these conversations and troubleshoot accordingly. Never talk s*** about other direct reports in a 1:1—it's a trap that's easy to fall into. Instead, acknowledge that roles are complex, and then make a mental note to get to the employee in question gracefully and evaluate how you can assist.

A good 1:1 performance by you as a manager of people is equal parts empathy, career agency, and feedback . . . preferably in that order.

Tool 24: How to Set the Right 1:1 Expectation and Vibe with Your Employees

If you're brand new to the game or simply looking to refresh/ reinvent your approach, here's some base language to use to set the expectation for how the 1:1 will run with your direct report:

> "Hi Tricia, to level set on how our 1:1s will work, I'd like our time to be totally focused on what you need from me to be successful. With that in mind, I'd like you to come up with at least three to five things you'd like to talk about each time we meet. Topics can be anything. Examples can include progress you're proud of, areas where you need my help, people you'd like me to nudge on your behalf, etc. Whatever you need help with or things you think I need to know are appropriate topics. I'll only hit items on my mind after we move through your list and if time allows."

Customize that for your brand, adding exclamation points to denote being pumped consistent with your level of extroversion.

Tool 25: The Perfect 1:1 Agenda and Flow

Once that's done, *here's my recommendation for a perfect 1:1 Agenda & Flow* where you touch all the bases to support your direct report, be a true Career Agent, and get what you need as a manager:

1. **Run through the employee's list.** The core of any 1:1. Knock down barriers, give feedback, help them establish Burst Goals to break down projects that seem insurmountable, etc. You'll spend the most time here, and you'll flow into many of the things that follow on this proposed agenda naturally as you help them troubleshoot.

2. **Hit a developmental conversation with the employee.** What are they working on that's growing them for the future? At times everyone loses sight of this, so it's a good idea to be purposeful to talk about their growth.

3. **Talk about people in the employee's circle of influence.** Politics people! Whether it's people on your direct report's team (if you lead other managers of people) or the aforementioned blockers, talking about how to influence others in the organization is always an elevated play for you as a leader.[5]

4. **Discuss what you're working on.** Take them inside the curtain. Talk a bit about what you're working on to give them an update. They'll appreciate the reciprocity and feel like a peer as a result. This doesn't have to be more than five minutes, but it matters.[6]

5. **Hit some Q&A with the employee on their goals and deliverables.** You're a sneaky one. You hit their list, talked about their development, people you both know in your company, and even what you're working on before you

---

5. Nothing makes your employees love you more than good advice on how to deal with difficult people.
6. If you're managing a Natural/star, asking for their take on something you're working on is engagement/retention gold.

hit them with the following type of question: "Where are you at with the Penske account?" Most of the time you'll already have the answer, but in case you don't, following up on some items important to you comes last. You earned that right by making the rest of the 1:1 up to this point 100 percent about *their* needs.

Follow this agenda and flow, be flexible yet consistent on the need to meet, and you'll do 1:1s better than 90 percent of your peers.

Don't forget to close positive. Natural, Aspirational, or Misfit, your people love to hear the fact that you believe.

KD'S CHEAT SHEET:
1:1 MEETINGS WITH DIRECT REPORTS

DO THIS!
○ Book 1:1s with each of your direct reports weekly.
○ Book an hour for each 1:1 with direct reports.
○ Set the expectation the employee will lead the session with what they want to discuss.
○ Use the time to probe deep into what's preventing your employee from being successful and seek to help them.
○ Talk about realities related to organizational politics as a method of helping your direct report be successful.

WATCH OUT FOR THESE TRAPS!
○ Don't cancel 1:1s repeatedly, but don't be afraid to mutually agree with your direct report to skip one occasionally if you're both all caught up.
○ Don't use the whole hour if you don't need it. When you're done, you're done.
○ Don't get impatient and simply start going down your list before the employee has a chance to lead.
○ Don't outwardly judge your direct report for places they are struggling. Help them!
○ Don't trash others in your 1:1. Acknowledge blocking behavior and seek to help your direct report get past the barriers without disparaging comments.

RESOURCES FOR YOU ONLINE - BESTBOSSEVER.ORG
○ 1:1 Checklist/Agenda
○ Sample copy for invite to initial 1:1 to set the stage for format and expectations

 KRIS DUNN

15

Shout Outs Are Really Just Smoke Signals from the Vatican (Recognition)

The craving for recognition is every artist's Achilles heel.
—Marty Rubin

In the earlier chapter on my Six-Step Coaching Tool, I said, "If you need multiple chapters on coaching positive work, you've bought the wrong book."

I didn't lie.

In this spirit, I bring you *one* chapter on recognition, packed with observations the deplorables among you will inherently understand but the engagement establishment will admonish me for.[1] I'll dig deep for you, but the TL;DR version of this chapter is as follows:

> Awards and formal forms of recognition are the opiate of the masses.[2]
>
> Real-time recognition that feels organic from a manager is what builds true gravity.

It's not that awards and other expected recognition tools are bad, it's just that they are ultimately average. From employee of the month to software solutions that allow you to instantly recognize

---

1. No politics in my definition of *deplorables*, which is "people who like to stir s**t up and zig when others zag."
2. When thinking of sleepy practices designed to keep the masses happy, I always go Karl Marx. #*Pravda.*

your teammates and (gasp) earn rewards points for doing so, the expected gears and institutions of recognition always revert to the mean—which means over time they are ignored by the masses.

You know what's never ignored by anyone in earshot? *A seemingly hot but positive take on what someone did on the team delivered with spice.* It's science—people are always going to weigh the informal conversations as more truthful than the scripted.

Should you still do formal recognition? Of course, but if that's all you do as part of your recognition strategy as a manager, you're as stale as the bagel that Eddie from accounting has had by his keyboard for the last four days. Get your act together, Eddie.

You Should Do All the Formal Recognition Programs but Be Better than Your Peers

Whatever the formal recognition program provided by your company, you should participate. *Employee of the Month/Year* and *Annual Values Champion* are examples of some of the big-box programs you'll see, and many of you have the opportunity (as do all employees) to participate in a recognition system that allows you to formally recognize your team and others any time you wish.

Where ongoing formal recognition programs fail is the expectation that they're forced. Most people use unlimited recognition systems consistently at launch, only to forget they are there. Automated emails sharing system-based recognition at your organization become white noise, deprioritized and unopened for days like the 50-percent-off email from Old Navy.

Use the recognition programs provided to their full extent, my citizens. Then share the formal recognition you did via some of the *informal* ideas I'll share through the rest of the chapter.

Average managers use these formal recognition programs and think their job is done. Managers who see the game know these programs aren't enough.

Tool 26: A Checklist of Where to Use
Real Time/Organic Recognition
Real Time Recognition + Sharing = Winning

What's better to an employee than a fake crystal award or an email showing that someone in the organization took thirty seconds to name you a "game changer" via a saved login and three clicks?

You guessed it, feedback from you, their manager, delivered in real time and in an authentic way that suggests you believe they crushed something of importance.

There are many ways to deliver this real-time, positive judgment on your direct reports with impact. The list of ways to share the good news organically include the following:

» **On the fly.** As mentioned elsewhere in this manual for the manager life, "when you see it, say it." The most powerful form of recognition is the quick hit version, where you give positive vibes in real time using informal language, explain the value you witnessed, and say thanks for a job well done. You don't prepare for this or write a justification. It's you and the talent in front of you. Note this is usually done face-to-face, but text provides a great way to cut through the day's clutter and get to your remote employee in real time as well. Emojis work as well, but only if "on brand" for you.[3]

» **In a 1:1.** When your direct report is running through the good, the bad, and the ugly in a 1:1, there's no better time to spot up with some positive feedback. This is a deeper connection point than the "on the fly" version of recognition, as you can tell someone how they nailed a situation or a project in a 1:1 and dig in a bit regarding why their approach or performance was so good. It also sets you up nicely for "good to

---

3. If on brand, there's still the question of which specific emojis to use. If you're not a volume emoji user, find a local consultant (Gen Z) for counsel before flowing the goat emoji out to someone.

great," with the recognition providing the spoonful of sugar that helps the medicine (you want even more from them in the area in question) go down.

» **In mixed company.** BALLER ALERT. Great managers are unafraid to recognize and provide specific praise for their direct reports around others. Understanding the psychology of recognition, they see the power in simple statements like, "Did you see what Janice did with the Singer account?" when Janice *and* a person of influence are in front of them. The organic conversation that follows inside this group of three raises the impact of recognition exponentially.

» **In a team or otherwise large meeting.** PRO MOVE. You're in a meeting and you hear something tangentially related to Janice's work on the Singer account, so you mention the work, giving a quick description and a shout out to Janice. Whether it lasts thirty seconds or five minutes (because others want to talk about it), you win. Note this type of recognition insertion is organic and more powerful than you formally recognizing Janice at the start of the meeting. The formal is good, the informal/organic is great. Be great.

» **Via an email** (bonus points if you're forwarding an email and commenting). You get two hundred emails a day because you're the boss. Recognition via email that you create from scratch is good. Forwarding another email and adding your comments, then sharing it with the employee in question AND others is great. Think of these as you retweeting the work of others (their email) and repurposing it for your recognition needs. You've become a curator of other people's email for your needs and are achieving recognition nirvana via the smallest time investment possible. BRILLIANT.

These organic forms of recognition/positive feedback matter more than formal recognition programs. But to truly self-actualize your recognition powers, you need to add some flavor to the proceedings.

Tool 27: How to Add Spice to Your Recognition for Greater Meaning

Variety is the spice of life, but *color commentary and context is the spice of recognition.*

Say what? One of the problems with formal recognition is that it sits on something resembling a two-dimensional plane. Recognition is provided with an explanation of the accomplishment in question. Golf clapping ensues,[4] and we're back to email or the departmental meeting.

Real time/organic recognition provided by a manager via one of the scenarios listed in our earlier list can be something more. You're still saying "great job," but the informal setting allows you to take your employee *inside your true thoughts and emotions* about the great performance you've witnessed.

I call these inside thoughts "spice," and they can include the following contextual points to your recognition:

» **All the haters who were blocking the employee from succeeding.** Organizations (to say nothing of the outside world) are full of blockers who can prevent your employee from getting great things done. Saying words like, "They didn't want you to succeed, but you got it done!!" or something more specific can never be said publicly. But in a 1:1 or small group setting, you can acknowledge the barrier of others blocking as a leader.[5]

» **How the accomplishment positions the employee for the future.** When's the last time you read the following in formal recognition: "*William continues to kick a** and let's face it, he's looking really good from a career perspective at our company*"?

---

4. Your employee gets a little bit of warmth from this polite organizational applause, but no one will ever know how they really wrestled an alligator to the ground to get the sought-after "Cares for the Customer" badge. Sad!
5. Every organization of any size has internal "us versus them." Celebrating the defeat of haters must be acknowledged, and you're the only one who can do it for your people. Acknowledge the blockers, celebrate the wins, and move on.

You can't say that in formal recognition, but versions of this spice are a natural add in your real time/recognition as a manager of choice.

» **What the accomplishment means for the department or you as a manager.** Sometimes an employee doing good helps others get more done or be positioned more positively as a result of the accomplishment. Acknowledging the win for everyone made possible by the employee in question is a great way of saying thanks.

Think of *recognition spice* as all the things you want to say in a formal announcement but can't. These opportunities for context and deeper meaning are why great managers always practice real time/organic recognition on their own in addition to formal recognition programs.

Candor = influence = engagement = performance and retention. This is why you should always do recognition beyond the formal programs inside your company.

Your Recognition Game Should Be Selfish and Must Include Good versus Great

We end this primer on real recognition for your people with the following note: *you do real-time/organic recognition because your employee deserves the warm glow and kudos, but you also do it because it's strategically selfish.*

Selfish?[6] Yeah, selfish.

Recognition done the way I've described matters because it gives you better retention as a manager.

More importantly, going deep on real time/organic recognition is the path to even greater future performance. By going deep on your own personal retention strategies, you're celebrating everything

---

6. "How dare you think of your own needs, KD."

the employee has done well, which sets you up to ask for even more via the "good to great" strategy discussed in the performance management section of this book.

Every conversation you have with your people is either a withdrawal or a deposit.

Make deposits with your people that others can't or won't, and you win as a leader.[7]

KD'S CHEAT SHEET: RECOGNITION

DO THIS!
- ○ Participate willingly in formal recognition programs regardless of limitations.
- ○ Use formal recognition awards as part of your own real-time/organic recognition strategies.
- ○ Use real-time/organic recognition, crafted by you, on a regular basis.
- ○ Use a variety of communication techniques to tell your personally crafted recognition stories for maximum effect (email, 1:1s, broader meetings).
- ○ Dig deep and add spice to your recognition, identifying the real reasons the work in question was stellar.

WATCH OUT FOR THESE TRAPS!
- ○ Never assume that formal recognition programs are enough.
- ○ Don't avoid providing recognition for great work by rationalizing it will embarrass someone or make others feel bad/be jealous.
- ○ Don't forget that a quick text to someone, while not public recognition, can make their day and at times is as powerful as broader communications.
- ○ Don't spray recognition out to multiple people on a daily basis. If you go overboard, recognition can lose its impact. Find the middle ground between not enough and too much.

MORE FUN STUFF ONLINE
- ○ Video clips of Jason Bateman providing positive recognition to Will Smith in *Hancock*, both in a 1:1 and publicly

 KRIS DUNN

---

7. Many of your peers won't give deep organic recognition out of a misplaced need to treat everyone equally and to not create the appearance of favorites. Remember this is the vibe of an average leader. Don't let the average people drag you back to the pack.

16

Why Grunt Work Is Good for Your Career
(WIIFM)

> *The thing is, Bob, it's not that I'm*
> *lazy, it's that I just don't care.*
> —Peter Gibbons in *Office Space*

Billy!!!

Everybody liked Elaine, especially her team of seven direct reports. Always warm, personable, and likable, she had seen a lot of success in her first two years as a manager of people.

Billy (aka William: informality was part of Elaine's brand) was one of three direct reports that needed the most attention from Elaine. At times, Elaine felt like she was Billy's personal organizer, as the attention level needed to get Billy's performance to a base level far exceeded that needed from others.

The time commitment wasn't a big deal for Elaine. The real issue was that Billy floated to things he enjoyed or considered himself good at, and didn't get the work he considered less prime done unless Elaine absolutely badgered him about it and asked him about it three times.

Elaine arrived at Billy's cube and launched into the small talk she loved. She put the secret timer on in her head that would tell her when it was okay to ask about the manual report Billy had promised *for the third time.*

As she listened to Billy talk about the new Netflix series he was bingeing, Elaine daydreamed about how cool it would be to just rip into him and tell him she was going to fire him if he didn't manage his work better.

Then she told him what *she* was watching on Amazon Prime.[1] The dream was dead.

There's Always a Middle Choice between Intimidation and Constant Hugs

In every life, some drudgery must pass. *Translation: Parts of your job really suck.*

Of course, you're in charge as a manager of people. What really matters is how you engage with your people when you ask them to do (1) things they really would rather not do and (2) more than they are currently doing in a specific area, even if their performance level is good.

Some managers are hard on others. Some people (like Elaine) try to exclusively use logic and care to migrate their employees to a better place. The theme of this entire book is about finding the middle ground, being direct and honest with employees while treating them with respect, and helping them see what is possible when they take accountability for outcomes.

You know, be a real person.

Whether you're dealing with a "Billy" (not doing things he doesn't want to do) or trying to get next-level performance from someone who's already a good performer, I always recommend you find the Career Agent voice inside you and use the *WIIFM method.*

What the hell is WIIFM? It's you starting every conversation from the lens of the employee.

---

1. But less enthusiastically than normal, given her tough love daydream. That'll show Billy!!

Let's Start with a Definition of WIIFM and Some Examples

Let's go to the true authority (Urban Dictionary, of course) for a definition of WIIFM:

> **WIIFM**
>
> Acronym for "What's in it for me?" A question that may be asked about a new idea or method where the benefits are not obvious.
>
> *"That new app looks nice, but really, WIIFM?"* [2]

The example used before notes the fact that new products and services use the concept of WIIFM the most in the business world. After all, who really knew that they needed a supercomputer (i.e., smartphone) in their hand to use five hundred times a day before it was invented?

> "I'll never give up this Motorola flip phone for that expensive, impractical Apple thing." [3]

WIIFM is needed when adoption is questionable and not a given. It's easy to move from the world of products and services and see the need for WIIFM in your daily interactions with your employees. Consider the following situations where employee belief, adoption, and desire to do something you need them to do (looking at you, Billy) is often low/questionable at best:

» Using the systems you provide them consistently.
» Doing grunt work they hate.
» Having a difficult conversation with a coworker.

---

2. Urban Dictionary, s.v. "WIIFM," accessed July 15, 2022, https://www.urban-dictionary.com/define.php?term=WIIFM.
3. Substitute "Nokia" if that was your boomer/Gen X jam rather than the StarTac.

» Getting more organized because they're missing things.

» Influencing and communicating to a cross-departmental manager at a level above their position on the org chart.

» Doing more than the minimum/seeking to add value in an area of their job they're not comfortable in.

» Giving a presentation when they aren't comfortable speaking in front of groups.

The list of similar possibilities is endless. You want to just tell them what to do in each of these areas and move on. But to be a true manager of choice, you've got to tell them what's in it for them (WIIFM) as a means of getting them to take action and to see the value in the activity for themselves.

Tool 28: Places to Insert WIIFM into Conversations with Employees
There's Always a WIIFM, You Just Have to Find It

What's in it for your employee to get better in areas you talk to them about? To have quality WIIFM conversations, you have to understand how to frame WIIFM, whether it's an entry-level task or you want them to go after a BHAG.

Cliff notes for positioning WIIFM in specific areas appear next:

» **Activities that suck.** Framing includes, "I wouldn't want to work on that either, but if you don't get it done you're going to put yourself at risk," and "You can't really get to the work that is going to drive your career until you knock the base stuff out."

» **Giving three s**ts in a specific area.** Same talking points as #1, with the exception that you're generally dealing with an average or above-average employee. Care more about the small stuff or the things you hate, so you can keep your job and/or do more of what you love. The three s**ts conversation means that it's less about one specific thing, as in #1, and more of a lifestyle choice from the employee.[4]

» **Getting people to hate you less.** When the overall work is good and few gaps exist, but people absolutely hate your employee, the WIIFM talking points include, "We need you to be better on the relationship side of the house so you can do everything you want here at ACME," and "I'm concerned someone is going to shank you in the parking deck."[5]

» **Going for big wins when they just want to watch Hulu.** When everything is good (they're keeping their feet on the ground) but not chasing big wins, BHAGs, or value-added work (not reaching for the stars), you provide good-to-great feedback and tell them why chasing great performance is good for them, their family, and the planet.

Whether the feedback and ask is hard (get it together or perish, Billy) or soft (you should try to be great), WIIFM means you frame the conversation from the lens of the employee with a "survive" and/or "thrive" flavor.

Great managers always customize WIIFM.

Tool 29: How to Transfer the WIIFM Burden On Sucky McSh*tty Activities to the Employee

When I refer to the "Sucky McSh*tty" activities,[6] I'm talking about the grunt work that no employee wants to do. It's the data entry, systems compliance, or reporting type of items that suck the life out

---

4. An employee not giving three s**ts about entire areas usually means they are really good at a couple of things and feel empowered to blow off things they don't like. Interrupting that comfy place is your goal.
5. Substitute "cafeteria" or "nap pods" if you subsidize lunch, snacks, or meditation for your employee.
6. Trademark pending.

of someone's soul at work. But, of course, that work has to be done, so coach and prod as a manager you must.

How do you coach on the Sucky McSh*tty universe using the WIIFM method? Here's the talking tracks I've found to be helpful beyond simply telling them to do it:

» **That stuff really sucks, doesn't it?** Acknowledging the putrid nature of the tasks makes you human as a manager of people. You should say "it's BS we have to do this" as appropriate. #empathy

» **You have to do it or it will kill your career.** BUT, I can't help you my friend. It's part of the job, and by the way, I have my own list of turds I have to get done every week.[7] Welcome to Club Awful. I'm a member!

» **You could reengineer that stuff and do less of it across time if you were a baller.** Setup complete, here comes the left hook: the employee should think about ways to do this bad stuff more efficiently and spend less time on it. There's always opportunities to get the time spent in these areas down significantly if you try. "I'm happy to brainstorm your ideas, but I'm not going to tell you what to do. It's up to you."

» **I'll check in with you on the reengineering of the pile of suck and become less tolerant of your complaining over time.** Burden transferred, accountability clear. I told you to work on ways to get it done in less time or make it less of a burden, so let's discuss what you're doing in our upcoming 1:1s.

WIIFM conversations across the Sucky McSh*tty domain are about telling your employee they're responsible for figuring out a better way and spending less time on the crappy side of their job.

---

7. It's not a terrible idea to have two or three examples of things that suck in your job. No, you can't include this conversation as part of that list, but I like where your head's at.

Maybe they do reengineering, but maybe they just get the uninspiring work done because you said you wanted to chop it up on the topic in future 1:1s. Either way, you win.

The WIIFM on Asking Your Direct Report to Be Great Is Pure Upside

Using the WIFFM method with employees who are doing well is easy. It's the *good-to-great* feedback method discussed earlier, mixed with the vibe of you being the employee's Career Agent.

It's aspirational—the sunshine of your life as a manager of people.

> "I really like what you're doing in this area. Wouldn't it be cool if you could add X?"

"X" is the dream, the killer project or deliverable that fully engages the employee and helps them turbocharge their reputation and career. If the employee in question was an actor, it's the low budget but popular movie that allows you (the Career Agent) to put them in the equivalent of the next Marvel movie at your company.

Think Renee Zellweger and Matthew McConaughey doing *Texas Chainsaw Massacre: The Next Generation*, which allowed them to become, well, freaking Renee Zellweger and Matthew McConaughey.

The WIIFM for the stars is always about getting some visible great work done (no matter how low budget) then turning to what's possible and what's next.

Whether the Employee Believes Your WIIFM Vibe Is Their Choice

Not everyone is going to buy the WIIFM vibe you're laying down. That's okay. Remember our earlier conversations about the three profiles we discussed earlier: the Naturals, the Aspirationals, and the Misfits.

WIIFM for the Naturals is about setting them up for what's next, getting out of the way, and being available. The Aspirationals require an approach that focuses on the contrast of good versus great. Misfits require you to migrate them from being at risk to being merely good.

WIIFM is a key tool for managing the motivation of each profile type, but whether they follow is up to the individual. Some will, some won't.

Ending this chapter with a quote from Morpheus to Neo in *The Matrix* seems appropriate:[8]

> You take the blue pill—the story ends, you wake up in your bed, and believe whatever you want to believe. You take the red pill—you stay in Wonderland, and I show you how deep the rabbit hole goes. Remember, all I'm offering is the truth. Nothing more.

The blue pill is average career conversations and outcomes and you being indifferent as a manager, including periodic performance-improvement plans and 2 percent merit increases.

WIIFM/Career Agency is the red pill and what's possible if they commit to discretionary effort and a higher level of caring. The red pill is more than some can handle.[9]

Your job? To simply offer up the red pill like a decidedly less-cool version of Morpheus.

---

8. Of course, we can agree that the Wachowskis should have stopped with the first Matrix and not done the sequels. I'll be talking about the wisdom of career sequels with a Matrix theme in my next book. Preorder now.

9. Why would someone take the career equivalent of the blue pill? Because it's easier to bitch about the world than to chase great work.

KD'S CHEAT SHEET: WIIFM

DO THIS!

- ○ Look for opportunities to share WIIFM by seeking areas where your employees are underperforming.
- ○ Customize your WIIFM feedback by understanding if the direct report in question is a low, average, or high performer.
- ○ Have empathy in your approach—it's okay to admit that parts of the job suck.
- ○ Transfer accountability to the employee to find a better way to get the work in question done via focus, workflow, or reengineering the tasks in question.
- ○ Use the "good-to-great" contrast method to use WIIFM with high performers.

WATCH OUT FOR THESE TRAPS!

- ○ Don't avoid the conversation about an area where a direct report is struggling. WIIFM is the tool to help soften the dialog while remaining direct.
- ○ Don't treat all WIIFM feedback the same. High performers should get different WIIFM talking tracks than average or low performers.
- ○ Failure to follow up after the WIIFM conversation makes you look weak and hurts your ability to hold the employee accountable in the future.

 KRIS DUNN

17

When You Care So Much You'll Dare Them to Leave
(Building Portfolios)

Should I stay or should I go?
—The Clash

Mark had felt the queasy feeling before. More than once, actually.

As Natalia left his office, he had no clue whether she would still be part of the team in six weeks. All he knew at this point was that she had been approached for a job outside of their industry, but located just two miles away from their office in the Buckhead area of Atlanta.

He said the *quiet part out loud* after she was gone for twenty seconds: "****ing recruiters."

But as his eyes left the doorway and centered back on his desk, he saw the book that told him he was at least partly to blame for the current state of affairs. It was a *portfolio of Natalia's work* as a marketing manager at their company, and she had left it for Mark to review and comment on.

Mark opened his mouth and pretended to dry heave. He had no one but himself to blame.

Helping his direct reports promote their accomplishments had long been a part of Mark's philosophy as a manager, up to and including advice on putting together books detailing their big wins (called portfolios) so they never lost the story of the value they could provide.

To his best employees—the ones most valued and likely to be recruited—Mark always said he'd be happy to help them evaluate other career opportunities with no fear of retribution. It was part of his brand as someone everyone wanted to work for.

Natalia was leaning into that offer and expecting him to provide counsel, and by going so far as to share the portfolio she was going to provide to the other company, she was daring him to show fear.

As he picked up Natalia's portfolio, he noticed it was in full color and on a quality of paper unknown to their office.

Oh s**t. She was playing for keeps.

Let's Start by Defining What a Career Portfolio Is

Who's ready for a giant game of career chicken? Just me?

Also called a "professional portfolio," a *career portfolio* is a display or comprehensive collection of an employee's work.

Alternative names are the "brag book," the "look-at-me chronicles," and my favorite, the "leave behind." I like that last one because, in any normal interview, there's no way you can talk about all the things featured in the portfolio, so it has power as a way to tell people more about you after their time with you is over.[1]

Portfolios are commonly expected during the hiring process for jobs in the art, design, and publishing industries, and that's where I'm going to lose a lot of you. Just because your employees can use a portfolio in a job search doesn't mean you shouldn't promote it as a tool, and it's just as possible for an accountant to have an effective and dynamic portfolio as it is for a graphic designer.

---

1. The pro move is to drop your portfolio from four inches high on the desk/table as you're getting up to leave. If you've included enough, the sound will be a reminder to your host to check out the document. #Boom

Career Agents Recommend Portfolios to Everyone
But Only the Crazy Ones Care Enough to Execute

I think you should recommend that all your employees build portfolios of their best work (like Natalia).

"Easy for you to say, KD. You don't have to worry about me losing people to other companies."

Most of you are already a "hard no" on Mark's philosophy to help his direct reports evaluate other offers of employment, and you're a decided *WTF* about helping your employees build portfolios of their best work.

The dirty little secret to all of this progressive talk about being a Career Agent? Only your most talented employees are likely to *fully* utilize your willingness to invest in them.

Because *the work to become more valuable is hard.*

That's why talking about the value of a career portfolio isn't as risky as you think it is. Only your most valuable employees are going to have work that rises to the level of a portfolio, and only about half of those individuals are going to do the work to capture it as you recommend to them.[2]

When I think of the type of employee that will follow your advice to create a portfolio of their best work, I'm reminded of this ad from Apple:

> Here's to the crazy ones, the misfits, the rebels, the troublemakers, the round pegs in the square holes . . . the ones who see things differently—they're not fond of rules. . . . You can quote them, disagree with them, glorify or vilify them, but the only thing you can't do is ignore them because they change things . . . they push the

---

2. My experience as a recruiter shows that only 1 to 2 percent of professional-grade candidates have portfolios they share with hiring managers/executives.

human race forward, and while some may see them as the crazy ones, we see genius, because the ones who are crazy enough to think that they can change the world, are the ones who do.

Your stars will be the ones to naturally migrate to building portfolios because they seek work that has impact. They're looking to engage the world and share their work to grow and be around others like them.

You can either be part of that process or close your eyes and hope for the best. I say engage as a reminder who is *all-in* on their career. That would be you, by the way.

Tool 30: The List of Things Employees Should Include in Their Portfolios

If you do research on career portfolios, you'll find some boring recommendations on what can be included: résumé, other biographical information, list of skills, recommendations, and more.

Of course, that's the outside world talking. I would never recommend you help your star direct report put a résumé on display. Instead, you should focus your portfolio-building on helping them create a collection of their most meaningful and impactful work as part of your team.[3]

While creative types have the ability to create work portfolios with ease, almost any star in any functional area has the ability to create a strong portfolio of their work. To help your high-performing direct report create a portfolio item, simply think of a project they crushed/excelled in, and encourage them to capture the following:

---

3. Jedi Mind Trick: Tell them they don't need a résumé in your version of a portfolio because the value they'll show with your assistance transcends the industrial employment complex. Or just say, "Résumés are for average people."

» **Create a cover page providing a description and impact of the project.** This establishes the context of what they were trying to achieve such as a business problem. This is short (under two hundred words) with a lot of white space to make it uber-readable.

» **Show the final work product for the area in question.** While I've seen spreadsheets and other abstract tools used to show a star's work, a better solution for noncreative stars will be to develop a small presentation (think three to four slides via PowerPoint) to capture the work done and impact for your organization.

» **If available, show reactions and praise from internal stake-holders in question.** It's always good to see other people loving the high-end work that was completed. Your direct report may have to ask someone who loved their work to react in an email, which becomes perfect fodder to frame the project as a portfolio item.

If you're seeing a parallel to the STAR technique we covered in the interviewing and selection chapter of this book, you're an alert one! Any section of a career portfolio is attempting to (1) describe a situation of need, (2) talk about and show what they did to meet the need, and (3) describe what happened as a result (ample praise from the masses, improved metrics, etc.).

But KD, Portfolios Aren't a Fit for the Type of People I Manage

Oh, ye of little faith.

You might be right. But to truly evaluate whether you can help a person build a career portfolio, stop thinking about what they do for your company (the profession) and start asking if they're a star.

True stars always have an opportunity to develop portfolio items regardless of profession, because they're always looking to solve problems, add value, and make things better than they found them.

Let's take one of the most mundane white-collar professions we can think of—being a financial analyst! Many people would say that career portfolios don't make sense for this type of position. I'd counter that a star financial analyst has multiple areas where stellar work could provide the basis for a career portfolio, including (but not limited to) the following:

» Budgeting process
» Monthly variance analysis[4]
» Future projection modeling
» Headcount expense[5]
» Partnering with leaders[6]

The real question is not about the profession, it's about whether your star has added true value and made things better around them. If they have, they can likely pull together big wins/great work in many areas, and with your help, use my outline of the cover page/final work product/positive reactions to create multiple sections of a career portfolio.

Tool 31: How to Use Employee Portfolios inside Your Company

Stop worrying about whether a career portfolio is going to be used by your star to get another job.

---

4. I challenge you not to view value-added work in this area as sexy.
5. Most frequently cited project in this area—creating a "turnover factor" in financials.
6. Partnering initiative is necessary since the "turnover factor" project eliminated the slush fund of unfilled positions for leaders who miss revenue targets.

Instead, start embracing all the ways the presence of a portfolio process with your star(s) helps you as a progressive manager of people.

Ways that portfolios help you and your employee win internally include the following:

» **The Career Portfolio helps you promote your star to internal audiences.** Last time I checked, this outcome is good for both recognition and retention. Imagine your star developing a portfolio per my process with six killer pieces of work, followed by you being able to share that work with others over the next year inside your company.

» **Portfolios help build momentum for you to promote your people and get them paid.** A natural outcome of you sharing the impact of your direct report—they are more likely to get promoted and/or get paid more than their peers. You know what's good for retention? You guessed it: *a robust career path in your company and rising total comp.*[7]

» **Portfolios show the impact of your team to the business, which is good for your leadership brand.** You're making it all about the employee, which is awesome. This just in—if you have stars working for you, promotion of great work through portfolio items is good for your career as well.

» **Portfolio discussions help you with good versus great feedback loops as a manager of people.** Work that's simply "good" doesn't rise to the level of a portfolio. Portfolios become a descriptive way to help illustrate what great contributions look like.

---

7. The portfolio is also a great tool when you're attempting to get an annual increase for your star that's double or triple the company average.

C'mon Baby, Don't Fear the Reaper

Talent magnets don't worry about turnover and losing people. They understand their reputation as someone who builds careers and has a network of former employees doing great things inside (people getting promoted) and outside the company (sometimes people find great jobs elsewhere, thanks to your tutelage) is what makes them unique.

The best talent in any industry has been known to ask the following question:

> "Who used to be on your team who you now consider a peer?"

Career portfolios are a special tool for your best employees.

The impact of promoting the work of your stars is always greater than the fear of losing them.

KD'S CHEAT SHEET: HELPING EMPLOYEES BUILD CAREER PORTFOLIOS

DO THIS!

○ Offer up guidance on how to build a portfolio of great work to any direct report doing—wait for it—great work.

○ Be ready to guide the employee on what a career portfolio is, why it matters, and what actually goes in the document.

○ Contrast good versus great work as your method to illustrate what actually goes in a portfolio.

○ Use portfolio items created by your direct reports to promote their work aggressively inside your organization.

WATCH OUT FOR THESE TRAPS!

○ It's easy to be fearful that helping your employees display their best work will be used against you in the external job marketplace. Get over that fear and lean into the process.

○ Don't give into the stereotype that noncreative positions can't create career portfolios. It's all about displaying great work that solved a business problem or met a need.

○ Don't forget to help your employees clearly show the impact their work had on the business.

RESOURCES FOR YOU ONLINE - BESTBOSSEVER.ORG

○ Examples of Career Portfolios

 KRIS DUNN

Part IV

Winning

18

Who Died and Made You Queen?

(Manager Assimilation for New Teams)

*Do I need to be liked? Absolutely not. I like to be liked.
I enjoy being liked. I have to be liked. But it's not like
this compulsive need like my need to be praised.*
—Michael Scott, *The Office*

Change. Sometimes people just don't get it.

It was month three of Tabitha's tenure as a director of marketing at her Orlando-based company. As an outside hire into the management role, it was obvious that she was brought in to make change. New ideas, faster execution, and a different voice were the order of the day.

But a funny thing happened after the sixty-day honeymoon period in the new role. Tabitha's direct reports began to shut down and not engage or at times be belligerent to the new ideas she was bringing to the table. In addition, it felt like she wasn't really connecting with any of her seven direct reports and her stage banter—the easy, personal side conversations everyone has before you get down to business—felt forced and artificial.

The reactions from her peers were telling. "You really inherited a tough team" and "You'll get through it" were the most common refrains, although a quick evaluation of facial expressions as those words came out suggested they weren't sure.[1]

---

1. The head tilt and lack of eye contract as they said the last phrase was the dead giveaway; poker players they were not.

The company brought her in to move fast, but she felt like her ideas and leadership weren't being valued by the team she inherited.

Maybe she made a mistake with this career move.

Tabitha Missed One Thing: She Didn't Run a Manager Assimilation Session

There are hundreds of good reasons why new managers can struggle in new roles: tough business, under-resourced, too many things to fix, etc.

All of these struggle points are all the more reason for managers to rationalize moving fast and telling people what needs to happen as part of any new team they've inherited.

After all, if the probability of failure is more than a rounding error, and if your experience tells you with certainty what needs to be done, the smart option is to move with blinding speed, right?

Yes and no. You've got to move fast, but not at the expense of real onboarding for your new team. True trust—the kind that can't be demanded through your position in an organizational chart—starts with you being secure enough to be vulnerable in your introduction to your new team.

Enter the *Manager Assimilation Session*, defined here as a simple session with you and your new team where the whole objective is to get them more connected with what makes you tick in a transparent way. Here's my basic definition of what you're trying to accomplish with this session:

- » **Provide direct reports with the opportunity to "get to know" their manager** (that's you) in a very short period of time.
- » **Begin to build the basis for a longer-term working relationship** between the manager and their team of direct reports.

» **Lay the foundation**, very early on, for open communication and problem-solving between the manager and their direct reports.

Ideally, the Manager Assimilation Session should be conducted within your first two weeks in the new role. Booking and conducting the session as early as possible in your tenure with a new team is critical to a fast but sustainable start.[2]

Tool 32: Your Manager Assimilation Session Project Plan

If you're still reading this chapter, you've accepted the fact that being emotionally humble and vulnerable early with your new team is good for you in the long run. With that in mind, we offer up the following project plan to get your Manager Assimilation Session planned and executed in five easy steps:

1. **Pick and secure a third-party facilitator.** You can't lead the session (duh), it has to be someone more neutral. You don't have to go outside the company, but the person you pick to lead the session shouldn't be your best friend and should have decent facilitation skills.

2. **Decide what you want to cover in the session.** The right mix is a balance of digging in on what makes *you tick* as an individual/manager/leader and *what they want/need/fear* as new members of your team. Letting them see and interact with you on your assessment profile is a good start, but you'll need to cover some other things as well. Try to not make it all about you. See the section that follows for a list

---

2. Assume people are talking about you from day one. The longer it takes you to do this session, the longer you're subject to "hot takes" on what makes you tick and your motivations. Unverified hot takes early in your tenure are rarely complimentary, BTW.

of potential activities during the session. Expect to spend at
least two hours in the session.

3. **Invite your new direct reports to the session and tell
them what you're trying to accomplish.** This is the intro
to the session and to the facilitator, as well as any prep the
facilitator would like your team to do for the session. The
intro should push all questions/info requests to your facilitator so participants feel a spirit of confidentiality.[3]

4. **Run the session.** You're basically having your facilitator go
through the list of things you sent out with specific focus
questions the team has for you and what makes you tick as
a manager mixed with your assessment profile. Your job is
to show up, not be threatened by the proceedings, and be
engaging.[4]

5. **Send out a recap of what you learned to the team.** What
did you learn in the session? What does it mean for how
you'll work together as a team? What was the most embarrassing question to you? You'll want to send out a recap that
focuses on the interactions you had, and what both parties
(you and the collective team) learned about each other.

Most of you want nothing to do with this type of Manager
Assimilation Session.

I get it, but to win you're going to have to be vulnerable. Everything
we've been taught about being managers of people says, "Stay
strong." But failing to dig in on what makes you tick and the team's
hopes and fears early in your tenure is a missed opportunity. Think
of this session as a down payment for stronger relationships with
your team.

---

3. "Please CC me when you send confidential questions to the facilitator." LOL.
One of you actually thought this!
4. Yeah, most of you will have to fake not feeling threatened by this. Tough,
sucks to be you. Think of it as a flu shot for your career.

Tool 33: Things to Include in Your
Manager Assimilation Session

The items you could include for review and discussion in the Manager Assimilation Session are endless. To make good use of the group's time together, remember this rule of thumb: the Manager Assimilation Session is not a replacement for you digging in with individual direct reports in separate sessions and 1:1s. Instead, it's designed to help you and your direct reports get to know each other and avoid paranoia and early misunderstandings.

More importantly, it creates an environment/open setting where everyone hears the same thing on important topics. This matters because it reduces the influence of people who want to block your success (for a multitude of reasons). It is harder to block you as the new manager when everyone is together, and you don't look evil.

With that in mind, some good things to include in your session include the following:

» **A list of important questions your new team has for you and what they want you to know about them.** What do they know about you? What else do they want to know? What are their concerns in the transition? What do they need most moving forward? Best practice is for your facilitator to do pre-work with the team to build the list of questions (through email or a stand-alone session without you) and cover these live, let you react, and let them add commentary as part of the session. You simply connect, show your empathy and understanding of the issues, and be human and approachable.

» **Digging into your behavioral assessment profile.** We all have a preferred work style that's driven by our behavioral DNA, so it's a good idea to ask your facilitator to share your assessment profile and drive a conversation about your managerial strengths. Bonus points for you interacting in a balanced form, talking not only about strengths but also areas in which you've worked to improve based on your profile.[5]

»   **An AMA about you.** The "Ask Me Anything" section is a great way to let your new team freestyle questions to you, including personal items about hobbies, family, how many days a week you drink, etc. The more you give candor in the initial questions you hear, the more follow-up questions that will be asked.[6] Your facilitator can help prime the pump here as well, either on the fly or via prep with the team before your live session.

»   **An AMA about them.** Who here loves "active listening?" Just me? I kid, but a great end to the Manager Assimilation Session is for you to ask smart questions to the group based on the quality interaction you've had in the session. Your AMA questions to the group should be follow-up questions to what you've heard that focus on what the group needs moving forward. That shows you're listening and, at the end of the session, making it more about them than you.

Add to this format at will and go have a great session. Remember, while you're the focus of this session, having a chance for increased trust and communication is all about transparency and approachability.

Who's not evil? You!

You'll Learn a Lot about Your Team, but the Big Win Is They Get a "Managed by Me" Manual

We interrupt this politically correct message of making your Manager Assimilation Session as much about them (your new team) as it is about you.

---

5. Of course, you're talking about areas you've tweaked and made adjustments to get better, not the "anchor around your neck" issues that caused you to be fired in your last job. Just clarifying.
6. You'll learn a lot about your team based on who engages and how they interact as free-flowing dialogue occurs.

It's still mostly about you.

At their best, Manager Assimilation Sessions are an owner's manual of sorts—a "managed by me" tutorial. You want to hear about their needs, fears, and misses from the past. But at the end of the day, you're still there to help the team perform at the highest level possible.

If your new team doesn't get the "managed by me" notes on what's most important to you and what to expect in interactions with you, you've missed the point of the session. Whatever features are a part of your manager brand ("I love digging into what you're working on so I can help"[7] or "I want everyone to have a stretch goal that drives their personal growth"[8]), the session needs to set the stage for what's to come.

Go thread the needle. A great Manager Assimilation Session is equal parts listening and expectation setting on your style.

---

7. Code for "I'm going to drill down so deep you're going to think you're running an oil project for BP."
8. "Can the superstars on my new team just raise your hands so I can write down your names?"

KD'S CHEAT SHEET:
MANAGER ASSIMILATION SESSIONS

DO THIS!

- Try to run your manager assimilation process in the first two weeks on the job (certainly within the first month).
- Find a facilitator for the live meeting. You'll need someone with the right skills and they can't be a good friend of yours.
- Set up the process with the facilitator (info requested before the meeting with a confidentiality clause) and remove yourself from the prep process the facilitator runs with your team.
- Show up on game day (day of the meeting) humble, ready to participate, and incredibly honest and transparent for the new team.

WATCH OUT FOR THESE TRAPS!

- Don't believe the voice in your head that says you don't need a Manager Assimilation Session. If you have that voice in your head, you're likely to be the one who needs the session the most.
- Don't make the session all about you. Have a 50/50 split between exercises that help the team understand you, as well as a block that helps you understand the team's current state of mind.
- Don't think that the Manager Assimilation Session solves all of your onboarding-to-the-team problems. Use it as a launch point for great conversations with individual team members, digging deeper in 1:1s for greater understanding and connection.

 KRIS DUNN

19

How to Tell Jeff Bezos He's Wrong (The Art of Managing Up)

Sometimes you just have to put on lip
gloss and pretend to be psyched.
—Mindy Kaling

Another week brings another mediocre 1:1 with the boss.

Sharon was used to this by now, but she still resented the feeling. After all, Sharon had a big job as a manager of customer service inside a huge call center, and her years of experience with the company should buy her a little grace, right?

Brittney was Sharon's fourth manager in nine years with the company, and Sharon was tired of proving herself to new people. Brittney was graceful enough about it, and generally followed the 1:1 best practices playbook by allowing Sharon to drive the discussion until the end, at which time she'd ask about the status of some of the projects and initiatives important to her.

When Sharon had little progress to show on Brittney's priorities, it wasn't unpleasant, it was just awkward. Sharon would generally explain that the day-to-day grind consistently kept her from making progress on the extra things the boss wanted progress on. This seemed fine at first, but now, nine or ten 1:1s into the relationship, Brittney became less empathetic and decidedly neutral about the lack of progress.

Sharon hit the hallway for the elevator as soon as the 1:1 ended, thinking to herself, *She just doesn't get it; I wish she could do my job for a month to see how it goes.*[1]

An alarm as the elevator doors closed would have been appropriate for the situation.

Welcome to Club Rationalization/Low Situational Awareness

It's easy to say you're too busy to get to some things on your list. That happens to all of us. But all things on your list aren't created equal.

Sharon has fallen for one of the oldest unforced errors in the business world—not taking care of the boss and rationalizing that she's too busy to work on at least a couple of the boss's priorities.

Some bosses will just grind you up and demand you give them what they've asked for. That's actually the easy version of this equation. The real danger is the slow burn, where you are generally unresponsive to your boss's needs, and they give you space to figure it out. The space provided turns into disappointment over time, and you get coded as average or worse by your boss.

It doesn't matter how busy you are. The boss needs to be taken care of if you want to thrive in your career. It also stands to reason that they might actually have some good (or even great) ideas. That's why I'm on a mission of mercy with this chapter to give you the straight dope of the importance of *managing up*.

What's the Definition of Managing Up?

Managing up is a method of career development that's based on consciously working for the mutual benefit of yourself and a person

---

1. Another test: If you are actively asking yourself what your boss does all day, you're in a danger zone. If you are sharing that question with others, your career GPS reads, "Chernobyl."

of influence (most often your boss), and to work on things that you understand to be important (whether directly assigned or not) to that person of influence.

It doesn't mean avoiding work, kissing up, or trying to turn the tables on a higher-up, but instead understanding your boss's position and requirements and making yourself (and your team) known as a resource that can deliver results, execute broadly, and add value beyond what's expected.

Know the Difference between Managing Up and Sucking Up

If you hear "managing up" and think "sucking up," you've got a membership at Club Rationalization with Sharon. There's a lot of your manager peers who are part of the club.

If you have a boss, *managing up is part of your job.* It's good for you, but it's also critical for you to rep your team.

The leader who is not great at managing up is also less able to sponsor others, a less useful ally to their own team, and their team has to contend with a harsher, broader environment.[2]

If you won't manage up for yourself, you should do it for your team. WAKE UP.

Tool 34: Your Checklist for How to Manage Up
What Managing Up Looks Like in Real Time

Think lifestyle, partnership, and performance, not manipulation.

The cynic looks at managing up as a Dwight Schrute to Michael Scott–type play. But in the lexicon of managing up, forced compliments to a boss are nowhere to be found in the playbook. Instead,

---

2. This is the oft-forgotten "why" related to managing up and it's a bit sobering. There's always more on the line when you lead a team.

the aforementioned "working for mutual benefit" is the focus of managing up and includes the following no-brainer activities:

» **Work on the things that have been assigned to you with urgency and excellence.** We start our list of best practices in the world of managing up with an obvious one. When a person of influence (usually your boss—we'll get to broader definitions in a second) asks you to complete a task, start a project, or generally look into something, you should do it. Simple, right? The general rule of thumb is the clock starts ticking once the person asks. If they have to ask you more than once where you are with their project, you've lost. Be better than that.

» **Always be available.** And I mean always. Bosses and other people of influence in your company have needs. As it turns out, they got to where they are because they're not only talented but they also work extremely hard. When they work on nights and weekends and lob a question over to you, it's always in your best interest to respond to all requests (even ad hoc) like someone who has them prioritized. Sorry work-life balance thought leaders, that's the reality.

» **Make the influencers feel important and mentor-like.** Your boss and other influencers have knowledge and experience, and you can benefit from asking for advice and counsel that draws on their expertise.[3] Share your own thoughts in those conversations and be a good listener, and you're on your way to at least some type of mentor/protégé relationship. Smart play, but also a valuable play if you're looking to get better.

» **Make proactive recommendations.** If you're listening at all as your boss asks you to work on specific areas or projects, you'll have clarity to your boss's world view and priority list. Once you understand their priorities, the enlightened among you won't

---

3. Average leaders do what they think will work best. Above average to great leaders ask questions to understand what great looks like to those in power.

be afraid to make recommendations for improvement in the areas in question. Don't miss your shot.

» **Identify blocking behavior to the things that are important to your boss and other influencers.** You've been around the block and seen a few things, right? When an area or initiative is stuck, and you understand why, outline what you see and have a plan on how you can help if possible.

» **Kill said blocking behavior without being asked to.** Better yet, if within your control, kill the blocking behavior in question and report on what you saw and how you fixed it after the fact to the boss/influencer.

» **Communicate all of the above via my Framing chapter that follows.** It's not enough to do great work; you have to communicate it. Forest/trees, my people. The less assertive among you won't want to tell the world (bosses) what you did in the area in question, but it's a must if you're going to manage up effectively.

Those who are critical of the concept would be wise to look at the spirit of this list of managing-up activities. It's less politics and more mutual respect, collaboration, and the collective team kicking a**.

Know Who's Eligible for Inclusion in the Managing Up Metaverse

If the true definition of managing up is working for mutual benefit with those of influence, it stands to reason there are many targets related to managing up in your organization, including the following organizational coordinates:

» **Your boss.** Duh. The obvious one on this managing-up list is the person you should treat like an MVP and be most in synch with. They are also the one who will assign or nudge you in a specific area the most in your organization. Treat with respect and care, and don't take this person for granted. Think about your own direct reports and who treats you carelessly for perspective. That's a gut check on the current relationship you have with your boss.

» **Your boss's boss.** You'll hear from this person much less than your boss, but when they call, text, or email you, the urgency you feel should rival the submarine attack alarm in the movie *Red October*. There's long-term danger here if you treat this person casually because your opportunities to impress are limited.[4] Once an initial perception is set, it's tough to change.

» **Influencers elsewhere in the Kingdom.** You've got a career and a functional area. Influencers exist above your level in other departments and divisions, and they'll float in and out of your life. Managing up to this group can be a catalyst to great things in your career, as well as unbelievable business results and enhanced execution capabilities for your team.

» **Outside clients and customers that may drive perception of whether you're badass or not.** Depending on your industry, you may interact with clients who transcend your paygrade. The customer isn't always right, but they always should be managed up to. Urgency, action, and care are the events of the day here.

While your own boss is the primary target for managing up, many of the other characters will provide unique opportunities to raise your overall corporate approval rating. Your reality check is this: if you don't manage up to your current boss effectively on a week-by-week basis, you don't get and won't see the influence opportunity with the others I've described. So put the managing-up

---

4. Think Eminem in "Lose Yourself" from *8 Mile* when dealing with skip level leaders: "You only get one shot, do not miss your chance to blow." If this makes you nervous, sample this: "There's vomit on his sweater already, mom's spaghetti."

plan in place for your direct boss, and all else will fall into place over time.

Managing up is corporate muscle memory that you should seek to build over time.

How to Tell Your Boss They're Wrong
as a Part of Managing Up

Ah yes. At some point, having learned and practiced the art of managing up, you'll arrive at the juncture where you're considering telling your boss they're wrong on a matter of some significance. Look at you, all grown up! But proceed with caution.

Three things to check off before you give the proverbial "WTF?" to your boss:

» **You have to have done real managing up work to have the right to tell your boss they're wrong.** If you haven't made the time investment toward all the managing up activities we've described and made it part of your lifestyle, you haven't earned the right and shouldn't attempt to tell the boss they're wrong on any level. For context, remember our lead story with Sharon—she hasn't done the work and has no relationship currency to coach her boss.

» **Never tell your boss they're wrong or coach them in front of others.** Circle of trust, people. Managing up is, for the most part, a 1:1 activity. If you would ever consider coaching the boss in front of others, I've already failed with this chapter.

» **Pick your battles.** Do you really need to burn your powder about the way they ended that meeting? Make sure that you're coaching them on something of significance, and understand that at most, you have a couple of opportunities per year to break through and get them to listen and modify their approach/behavior.

At the end of the day, if you've done the hard work of managing up over time and you need to give hard feedback to your boss, there's only one way to approach it, and it sounds something like this:

> "Hey, I wanted to grab a couple of minutes and break down something I've been thinking about. I'm your biggest fan and feel naturally protective of you, and I think you're at risk with <insert issue> because <describe danger and the risk you see in detail>. I wouldn't bring it up if I didn't care."[5]

Put that in your own words, and you've got a chance to break through. But only if managing up is a feature of your professional lifestyle. If you've done the work and only play this hand occasionally, they'll appreciate they've got someone looking out for them and willing to tell the truth.

Managing Up: It's Not Show Friends, It's Show Business

Have no shame in managing up, because you're credible as hell and looking to do great things in tandem with those of influence.

The world wants you to be average. Don't listen to the haters who are trying to bring you back to the pack.

---

5. The safest path to telling your boss they're wrong is to tell them you have their back and are seeking to protect them from harm.

KD'S CHEAT SHEET: MANAGING UP

DO THIS!

○ Understand that what's important to people of influence around you has to be important to you and prioritize accordingly.
○ Be available and uber-responsive to those with influence and power.
○ Once you understand the priorities of those around you, make proactive suggestions and share information relevant to those priorities as a great team member.
○ Clearly communicate your efforts and wins to those of influence, especially in areas important to them.

WATCH OUT FOR THESE TRAPS!

○ Never confuse managing up with brown-nosing.
○ Don't witness blocking behavior toward initiatives important to your boss and do nothing. Work to remove the blocking behavior and tell your boss or those with influence what you're doing to make things better.
○ Don't limit your managing-up efforts to your boss. Understand you've got to manage up to others in your organization as well as to clients/customers.
○ If you aren't actively managing up, don't assume you have any currency to tell your boss that they are wrong or in danger. You have to do the work beforehand to build the relationship.

 KRIS DUNN

Bonus
Don't Call Me Fat during the Relo Trip

If you agree that managing up is smart for your career in any organization, I'd be remiss if I didn't mention there are other forms of influence that are equally important.

Example: *Let's talk about the art of influencing spouses/partners/significant others* connected to the lives of your employees! It's a form of managing down or across, if you will.

But why listen to me wax poetic about this when I have someone who is an expert?

Introducing my better half, **Angela Dunn**. Take it away, Angela, and shoot them straight.

I am married to the HR Capitalist, aka Kris Dunn. And yes, I call him that around the house; as in, "Hey Capitalist, dinner is ready." No, not really. I'm the boss, and he's lucky he gets to hang around.

Through the years, I've formed opinions (mostly good) about all of Kris's bosses, just like the spouses/partners/significant others of your direct reports do with you. Most of those opinions about you (the boss) are formed through casual talk around the house. But every once in a while, you'll get the opportunity to directly engage with the significant other of your direct reports and, in the understatement of the year, it's important that you're viewed as positive.

There is one absolutely true scenario in this area that we have experienced firsthand in Kris's career.

The year is 2001. We're living in Birmingham, Alabama, with our one-year-old son. Kris is a field-based VP of HR for a Fortune 500 that shall remain nameless. I am an assistant district attorney (that means I prosecute people who commit crimes) in an office I love and have some seniority, having been there for about four years. Kris gets the call from the higher ups to take a job in Denver, with said company, to lead the whole HR function for the western region of the United States. Neither of us have ever been to Denver, so the prospect certainly piques our curiosity.

So, Kris goes out a couple of weeks before me, interviews, and gets the official offer, makes the rounds in the Denver office, and does a little house hunting in his spare time. When he comes home, he issues me a very understated warning about the real estate in the metro and suburban Denver area, as in "Ang, the houses are not going to be quite as big or look like they do here. Just know that going in." Okay. He already realizes that selling this move to me was going to be difficult, so he is being sort of cautiously vague but definitely managing expectations. Anyway, we fly out there, and my initial illusions about beautiful, wooded neighborhoods are rapidly dismissed. We landed at the airport and it looked like the plains of Kansas—or the surface of the moon!

By this point, Kris is generally avoiding eye contact with me. On to the meet and greet! For lunch, we head to a local upscale Tex-Mex joint to meet up with the guy who would be Kris's boss in Denver if he were to accept this transition. Kris makes introductions and we sit down and order. Having never been to this restaurant, I order a salad as well as an entrée. When the food arrives, the servings and plates are HUGE and the salad and the entré are each on GINORMOUS plates of their own. Basically, three plates take up the whole table, and the waiter doesn't know where to put the fourth plate, which happens to be one of mine (I ordered a salad earlier, remember?).

As the waiter struggles to figure out where to put my second plate, the potential future boss looks right at me, no smile, and says, "Are you hungry, Angela?" in the most snide manner possible. Now, I have a fairly slim-to-average build (5'7", about 125 lbs.), and I don't easily get offended, but you have to admit that was over the top. I heard the air leave KD's lungs next to me; he must have been motioning for the check as he steadied himself from the dizziness.

Of course, that comment did not make or break our decision on whether to relocate to Denver, but for some people, it might have. Just imagine if I had been overweight and sensitive about it OR even worse, if I had been suffering from an eating disorder, like bulimia. What a ghastly mistake from the guy who should have been making his greatest effort to sell me, the spouse, on the relo.

Kris recovered in under two days and kept selling and had me convinced that we needed to go. Then, at the end of the process, he blinked and said he was going on "instinct" to not take the position and stay in his current role. What???

Eight months later, the Fortune 500 flew a plane into Denver and shut the divisional office down, taking the boss who cared enough to call the relocating spouse "fatty" (I'm making that up, but it feels good) out of the company along with everyone who reported to him. We would have been sitting in Denver eight months into the transition with double the mortgage and two fewer jobs.

The moral of the story for me as a spouse pondering relocation? Keep an open mind, take the trip, see the big picture, and at the end of the day, go with your gut, especially if the boss insinuates that your gut is large (which it was definitely not).

20

And Thou Shall Play Offense at All Times

(The Art of Framing as a Leader)

Never water yourself down because someone
can't handle you at 100 proof.
—Unknown

Marcy had been here before. So much so, it seemed like a mediocre movie that plays three times a week on FX—the kind you watch for fifteen minutes and end up hating yourself for getting sucked in.[1]

But today, Marcy wasn't watching the Stay Puft Marshmallow Man scene from *Ghostbusters*. If today's live scene was a Bill Murray movie, it would be *Groundhog Day,* because Stanley from engineering was bitching again to the group about his open positions while being careful not to make eye contact with her.

Marcy loathed the monthly ops meeting, because it always seemed to devolve into a conversation about how bad the recruiting function was. As the HR leader, recruiting was hers, and while the Stanleys of the world tried to not make it personal, she always left the session feeling like trash.

Recruiting in a post-pandemic world is challenging, and Marcy's team wasn't just sitting around, but credit was hard to come by. As she heard someone utter the hackneyed phrase "war for talent," her mind started drifting to the once unthinkable.

Maybe it was time for Marcy to slash the tires on Stanley's Ford F-150.

---

1. Most likely a "straight to video" classic from Melissa McCarthy or John C. Reilly.

Promote Your Good Work, My Humble Friends

Of course, if Marcy is good at what she does, she doesn't have to think about hurting Stanley by destroying the property he loves most in the world.

If you ever find yourself feeling self-pity like Marcy, ask yourself the following question: *Am I doing enough and seeking to add value with my team efforts and my own performance?*

If you look in the mirror and the answer is *yes*, you don't need another job. You need to be better at communicating your ideas, efforts, and outcomes via a process I call *framing*. Here's my definition:

> The most ~~talented~~ successful people in the world of work consistently *frame* their goals, work product, and outcomes *via varied communication strategies.*[2]

It's not enough to have a plan and work harder/smarter. You're going to have to be a marketer of your ideas to maximize your success as a leader and that of your team. If you don't tell people what you and your team are working on, they'll assume you're average. If you're better than average, you need this chapter.

So I'm Saying You're Responsible for Promoting the Work You Do, So What the #$!@ Is This Thing I Call "Framing"?

Framing is a lifestyle, with a specific philosophy and concrete actions. To do framing like the high-potential pro you are, you're going to use a variety of communication techniques to ensure everyone of

---

2. I crossed out "talented" but left it for you to see. The most talented among us aren't always the most successful, which is kind of what this chapter is all about.

importance knows what you're working on. Communication "must haves" include the following:

» **Communicating what your goals are for a specific period.** You're the leader, so don't make this mundane. Tell the people around you what big wins you're seeking and the s**t shows you're trying to fix.
» **Communicating your challenges and progress.** Updates people! Don't go dark. Keep peppering them with progress.
» **Communicating your wins and finished work product.** Wrap it up and deliver the good news. Also, if you failed, tell them why and what plan B is.
» **Communicating your opinions and takes on what's going on around you in your area of subject matter expertise (SME).** Who's the expert? You. So give them hot takes on all things that touch your SME practice.

To some of you, this seems like too much. I get it, but the big question you have to ask yourself is *whether you're going to let opinion about you and your team be created without your input, or whether you want to control the narrative.* The choice is yours, and for the HiPos reading this, there's only one correct answer.

Control the narrative.

Tool 35: The Five Rules of Framing Your Work

The art of framing can be summed up as follows: *Tell the people the good news.*[3]

The good news is that you and your team are 100 percent in control of things that matter to the business.

---

3. Proverbs 15:30. Also Vince Vaughn sharing the news he's starting a fraternity in *Old School.*

Whatever the area of focus or project, here's your roadmap for framing your work (or your team's work) like a pro:

1. **Always do a "behind the scenes" needs analysis.** This just in, taking the time to talk to people before you create meaningful work product shows you care. Asking influencers for their observations is key, and if you incorporate some of their thoughts into your project design, you're golden. The people you include in this stage are the pure influencers (senior leaders, key front-line people).

2. **Always provide launch materials for any project or recurring platform.** So you've got a great idea—sweet! We interrupt your excitement to remind you that if a tree falls in the forest, no one hears it. So, when launching something new, create launch materials that tell the who/what/why/how/where. The star of the launch materials (FAQs, timeline, and a cover note from you) is the idea and creator of the project, which of course is you (or a member of your team).

3. **Provide balanced updates on a consistent basis.** Once you launch a project, it's DOA if you never tell anyone how it's going, so update like your career depends on it. Analyzing struggles as well as celebrating success is a great way to build credibility. Updates usually come through reports and scoreboards, which are a great mechanism for pressuring people outside your team (those who have active roles) to support the project in question.[4]

4. **Close out project work with a win/loss analysis.** Adding value means putting yourself out there, which means at times you'll fail. Once a project has run its course, be brutally honest about the outcomes. The more you frame,

---

4. Remember Stanley from our opening story of this chapter? There's likely going to be a scoreboard that shows how quickly Stanley's team interviews candidates once submitted. Scoreboards motivate the right actions.

the more you'll become known as an innovator who's brave enough to report on and kill things that didn't work. Your successes will more than make up for the failures, and you'll be seen as a straight talker who takes action and gets things done.

5. **Use a variety of communications platforms to frame.** To be great at framing, you're going to have to be comfortable presenting what you're working on via email, presenting in meetings, 1:1s, and more. You can't rely on one medium. Don't forget your job as a framer across all communications mediums is to get in front of the message and *control the narrative.*[5]

Advanced Considerations for Framing like a Pro

Playing offense with effective communication is harder than it looks. To reach the graduate level of this class, consider the following advanced framing techniques:

» **Simply communicating more isn't enough to frame well.** Effective framers among top performers are always proactive versus reactive in their communications. BUT . . . they also have a style that makes communication from them seem like a mix of status updates, op/ed, and entertainment—it's not stiff and formal. Interrupting the pattern is key to the reputation you build as a proactive leader who gets stuff done.

» **Don't forget your team.** Help your direct reports under-stand the importance of framing as well. Lead by example and mandate they always have two big things they are work-ing on in addition to the grind (see MBOs and BHAGs in the goal-setting chapter). Use the Five Rules of Framing shared

---

5. Recommend the *Triple Play*, where you communicate the same info via decreasing detail and time across email, 1:1s, and team meetings.

previously to help them understand the value and teach them to frame as part of their role.

» **Great leaders target specific types of people when they frame.** The following audiences have different needs and are handled accordingly:

 › ENEMIES: Goal is for your framing to "mute" them, not convert them.[6]
 › FRIENDS: They already like you. Consolidating their support should be the goal.
 › FENCE-SITTERS: These are people who don't really have an opinion on you or your team. Your framing is the equivalent of a "drip marketing" campaign to raise awareness and perception.

At times, different audiences will need different forms of communication. The key to targeting these personas is that your framing is designed to influence over time, with primary targets being the fence-sitters (to convert them to fans over time) and enemies (to be so in control they can't be critical to your face or behind your back).

What Should Marcy Do? A Case Study on Framing

Our heroine from the start of the chapter has a recruiting issue. Marcy's in charge of recruiting, which isn't going great, but there's lots of blame to go around—in HR, but also in the line of business. Her HR and recruiting team are increasingly coming under siege for being a SPOF[7] for lukewarm recruiting and business results. Marcy

---

6. Enemies and naysayers LOVE IT when you don't frame. It makes it easy for them to create their own narrative about your work and at times to hide their own shortcomings. I see you, Stanley.
7. Single Point of Failure, otherwise known as "the one to blame."

isn't super-interested in recruiting but knows she needs to get in front of it.

Here's what Marcy knows:

» Her HR shop could be more focused on recruiting.
» She doesn't have enough resources to recruit effectively.
» Another part of the problem is that the managers she supports don't always have a sense of urgency to get positions filled.
» Recruiting is actually going okay in many areas, but she's getting chopped up by people who use her and her team as the reason they can't succeed.

Ready? Let's give Marcy a framing plan:[8]

STEP 1: Marcy goes on a "needs analysis" listening tour, primarily focused on meeting with leadership in the areas with the biggest recruiting need (as well as her own boss).

STEP 2: Marcy announces an initiative to cut the number of open positions in half, confident that she'll have the support of the leaders she met with in Step 1. She names the initiative "Project Greenlight" and announces her plan via email, ops meetings, and so on, and communicates it to all managers in the company/client group.

STEP 3: Knowing she's got a commitment from her boss that will allow her to succeed, Marcy develops three reports designed to provide balanced updates (the good, the bad, and the ugly). But, just as importantly, she's proactively getting her message out and not letting people use her or her HR team as an excuse.

Note that Marcy still has to perform against the plan. Average managers allow others to frame their performance, but good-to-great

---

8. Plan created by Kristian Patrick Dunn, life coach for struggling yet aspiring midlevel leaders currently being run over by peers in other departments.

managers understand it's all in their control and do great work, accompanied by great framing that helps them control the narrative for themselves and their team.

Marcy Effectively Framed the Project and Put It on Autopilot

Marcy is nobody's victim these days. Confident in her ability to get things done, she put herself on the line, communicated her plan, and provided updates via a variety of communication strategies: email, meetings, one-on-ones, ops meeting presentations, and so on.

Just as importantly, she got the following benefits from framing:

» The framing of the project and the reporting made Marcy treat the problem with more urgency and improved her performance.

» The updates she provided made it harder for people to use her and her team as an excuse.

» Because she got organized and overcommunicated, Marcy got new resources and budget spend approved to address the issues to a greater degree.[9]

» Marcy continued to use the reporting structure once the project was complete—to keep everyone honest and *proactively* show the work that was being done on a weekly basis.

Nobody talks about Marcy's inability to recruit for the organization anymore. Recruiting is now a priority for all to contribute to. Framing helped her win.

The best managers become their own PR firm when it comes to framing and controlling the narrative related to their work and the work of their team members.

Just do it. It's good for you.

---

9. One of the hidden benefits to framing is that when you get organized, have a plan, and start communicating, you're more likely to get funding to do great things. Funny how that works.

KD'S CHEAT SHEET:
THE ART OF FRAMING AS A LEADER

DO THIS!

○ If you're getting crushed in a single area, take control and do great work—launch a project to make that area better, have a plan, etc.

○ Communicate clearly through launch materials what you're going to do in the area in question, including FAQs, a cover note from you, etc.

○ Develop reports or consistent updates about what's going on in the area and give balanced updates on what's going well and where you're struggling.

○ Send your initial communications and reports/updates to all who matter—friend and foe alike—so everyone is clear on what you're doing and how it's going.

WATCH OUT FOR THESE TRAPS!

○ Don't simply accept blame for business conditions that happen to fall in your area but instead require cooperation and performance from individuals across the organization.

○ Failure to engage those who have been critical of your department/function at the start of the framing process is a mistake. The more you engage them and potentially use their ideas, the harder it is for them to remain critical.

○ Be careful about framing the launch of an initiative/approach, then failing to do great work in that area.

○ Don't forget to provide consistent updates on the progress of an initiative that you've framed.

 KRIS DUNN

Bonus

Are You a Jerk for Sending That Email at 9:00 p.m.?

Of course, framing and managing up (or down) has many layers. As important as *what* you communicate is *when* you communicate.

You being a total machine and working to get things done isn't the issue. The issue is the perception that you're projecting your workhorse mentality onto those who report to you who can't match your speed, urgency, or general kick-a** vibe.

In today's world of empathy, mental-health awareness, and work-life balance considerations, a growing population feels like you're part of the problem with your drive, ambition and . . . *after-hours emails*. Here we go! Buckle up!

A recent *Wall Street Journal* column cited a study of perceived urgency of after-hours emails. Here's what they found:

> We examined this question in a series of studies with a total of more than 4,000 working adults. We had participants take the perspective of either a sender or a receiver of a nonurgent work email sent outside work hours. We asked "senders" to indicate how quickly they expected a response and asked "receivers" to indicate how quickly they thought senders expected a response from them. We consistently found that receivers overestimated the need for a fast response—something we call the "email urgency bias."
>
> In both studies, we found that, on average, receivers assumed they needed to respond 36% faster to off-hours

work emails than senders expected. What's more, the receivers reported feeling more stressed by off-hours work emails than senders expected them to feel, and the stress associated with this unnecessary pressure resulted in lower subjective well-being.[1]

Without question, when a work email comes in after hours, a lot of your direct reports are going to treat it with more urgency. As they should, if you're the boss. The best practice is laying some ground rules for what you expect when you send the after-hours email.

But before we dig into that, let's further define the players in this email game of after-hours communication. Next is my roster of the players involved.

The Three Types of Managers When It Comes to After-Hours Email

1. **Fire away, let's get s**t done.** You might not expect an answer to your after-hours email. But you'll be damned if you're going to worry about how people feel when you send late night or weekend emails. By the way, I support you getting things done. Shine on, you crazy diamond. There's a reason you're in the seat you're in. The bottom line is if no one is sending after-hours emails, you probably don't have much of a company. Don't shoot the messenger, because it's true. "A" players aren't held captive by broad, overarching calls for normal office hours.

2. **I'm not sending this now, it will be seen as anti-work-life balance.** This manager has "seen the light" related to work-life balance and is not sending the message out when they think of it, making a note to send it out during

---

1. Laura Giurge and Vanessa Bohns, "The Curse of Off-Hours Email," *The Wall Street Journal*, October 2, 2021, https://www.wsj.com/articles/the-curse-of-off-hours-email-11633147261.

normal business hours. Is this rationalization? Is this the most efficient path? I could argue that many of these messages would be delayed by getting busy. In addition, managers who can say they never send out after-hours emails probably aren't—wait for it—working after hours! I could also argue that managers who don't work at least some after hours and weekends are on average trailing from a total production/results perspective. Again, don't kill the messenger. All things being equal, a manager putting in fifty-five hours is going to outperform one who works only normal business hours.[2] Hard facts from the salt mine of getting things done in high-pressure environments.

3. **I'm sending now but via Outlook's send later tool, so people think I'm cranking it out in the morning.** Ah! The evolved manager related to after-hours emails. This manager says the following: "*I'm here dominating after hours, but I'm aware that culturally, people are starting to be criticized for work-life balance signals with off-hours emails. I'm using 'send later' so people think my work day starts at 7:05 a.m.*"[3] This manager works when they want to work and, if they don't need the response immediately, is winning the game of public opinion by timing messages to be more palatable. They're still pushing the team to get things done; they're just showing that they are evolved, even if they wonder why others don't work the way they do.

But let's not forget the employee side of this after-hours email exchange. You can talk about work-life balance all you want, but the reality on the employee side is that some people are just built different—notes on which appear next.

---

2. No study cited for this claim. "School of Hard Knocks and Realism"
3. Note that I ran this by a leader who uses "send later," and she told me that she would never schedule the email to hit an inbox until an hour or two after the normal, society-endorsed workday start time. So nice as she grinds away at 9:00 p.m.!

The Three Types of Employees When It
Comes to Email Management

1. **I respond within the hour to anything you send.** Nights and weekends included. You love them. Maybe these folks do need to be protected a bit. But damn, it's nice to know they're there (Note: many Naturals from our earlier chapter fit into this persona).

2. **I don't respond during nights and weekends, but I'm in control and you aren't disappointed by my timeliness of response.** Cool. You still love #1 better, but you see this group and trust this group. We're good. Look forward to your response to the 9:00 p.m. email in the morning (Note: Naturals and Aspirationals from my earlier chapter populate this group).

3. **I have trouble being responsive to email.** It doesn't matter when it is sent; I'll rarely make you feel like you're a priority. The dirty secret to all the work-life balance world yelling about your after-hours emails is this: even if you send all your emails at normal times, this segment still sucks at responsiveness. They're also probably the first ones to bitch about your work ethic and drive, and yes, also about your 9:31 p.m. email about the McSurley account (you guessed it, this group is made of Misfits from our earlier anthropological tour. They've got bigger issues than your 9:00 p.m. email on a Tuesday).

Run through it, and your choices are clear. Keep doing what you're doing or adapt to a world that tells you to be kinder and gentler.

The *Wall Street Journal* article recommends making these disclaimers in your after-hours emails—I kid you not:

» "Even though I'm sending this email outside regular work hours, which fits my own work-life schedule best, I don't expect a response outside of your own work hours."[4]

» "Note that you might receive this message outside of my office hours but that I have no expectation to receive a message outside of your office hours."[5]

» "Please know that I respect boundaries around personal time. If you receive an email from me during your personal time, please protect your time and wait to respond until you are working. It's important that we all prioritize joy over email whenever possible."[6]

Geez. The problem with these messages is that you're still the boss, and you need service on the things you need service on. These disclaimers also rob your stars/Naturals of at least some motivation that they can outwork/outhustle their way to career success. You never want to create an environment where the people who want to outperform others don't feel like they have the opportunity to work how they want to work.

If you're concerned about all of this, I'd recommend the "send later" option. It still says you're working harder than most and need people to be in range of your sense of urgency. I'd text people as needed for immediate service on nights and weekends without making any of these proclamations.

The bigger the company, the more you'll need the strategy in this area in years to come.

Your employees' feelings matter. But then again, so do yours.

Don't let me interrupt your consumption of *Squid Game* with my Wednesday night email on saving a client.

---

4. "I'm a complete machine and looking to dominate. I understand if you aren't built the same way."
5. "Unless you want to. I'll be around (wink)."
6. I'm assuming the joy you're currently prioritizing is watching *Tiger King 2.* That's okay, I can wait."

Part V

Build It and They Will Come

21

Failure Is the New Black

(How to Build a Manager/Leadership Training Program)

I'm curious about other people. That's the essence of my acting. I'm interested in what it would be like to be you.
—Meryl Streep

If you're a leader with direct reports who manage teams, or otherwise hold broad responsibility for people management practices (HR, Learning and Development, etc.), you might be asking the following question:

"Do all my managers have the skills they need to be successful with their teams?"

Umm, yeah.[1] If you're asking this question, you already know the answer. Your managers are good at a lot of things, but they have room to grow when it comes to the concepts covered in this book.

Your instincts are telling you to get organized and provide training in the coming year for your organization's managers of people. Your instincts are 100 percent correct.

To help you get started, I'll provide some cliff notes here on what I've learned in putting thousands of managers through classroom and virtual training based on the concepts in this book.

---

1. Said in my best Bill Lumbergh (boss in *Office Space*) voice. Possible condescending tone alert.

First Understand That Your Definition of Leadership Matters

The first challenge you'll face when putting together a training series for managers of people is focus. If you're responsible for setting up programs for managers to learn how to manage, you'll automatically be drawn to broad leadership theory over core skills.

This move will be popular but misguided.

There's nothing wrong with high-level leadership theory. It's just that it exists in a stratosphere that's not actionable for the average manager of people. Training based on book titles like the following will be well received, but won't change actual behavior:

>> *Leaders Eat Last*
>> *Primal Leadership*
>> *The Hard Thing about Hard Things*
>> *True North*
>> *Blitzscaling with Your Team*[2]
>> *Lead from the Outside*

All of these titles are probably excellent books—they certainly have sold well. You could build training around any of these books and have an engaging session. Your team of managers will laugh, they'll cry, and they'll be introspective about the challenges the team faces in the coming year.

Then they'll return to the daily grind and have no idea what to do when one of their direct reports, Andrew, is bitching constantly about marketing and has caused a turf war that rivals the movie *Colors,* but featuring khakis and a mix of Macs and Microsoft Surfaces instead of guns.[3]

Fixing Andrew doesn't come from *Leaders Eat Last.* That's why you need to feature practical tools in any manager training you do.

---

2. Made this one up. The fact it didn't look out of place should make you go hmm.
3. Sean Penn will play Andrew in the movie about your team, just like he played a dangerous and disaffected Danny McGavin in *Colors.*

Map Out the Skills You Most Want to Grow in Your Managers of People

Organizational assessment time! Whether you're a learning and development professional or just plan on playing one on TV, it's time to do some gap analysis and determine what skills are lacking in your managers of people that prevent them from maximizing the success of their team.

To get out of the leadership theory realm and get to what's real, I recommend you start by *thinking about the ten most important conversations your managers need to have with the direct reports in a given year* and attempt to build training around that.

This book is my attempt to answer that question for you, which is why you see core chapters on *interviewing and selection, managing strengths and weaknesses, goal setting, coaching skills, change management, compensation,* and *performance management.*

Your list doesn't have to match mine, but steal what you can from my work and continue to add to it to match your needs.

Figure Out If You're Going to Buy Your Training Program or Build It

The "build or buy" question is next on your list of things to figure out. As a general rule, the more unique you think the culture at your company is, the less inclined you're going to be to buy manager training from an external provider.

Building your own program, of course, is full of landmines. You need the capacity to spend the time on the build, as well as the in-house expertise. What is the one thing going for you if you decide to build? *The more you strip the training down to the bare necessities, the more manageable the development cycle is going to be.* Taking some of the simple tools I've provided in this book and developing two-hour sessions around them is a great start and a path to success.

A hybrid approach (buy some modules, build some modules) also makes the development of manager training manageable as well, and lets your in-house team focus on what they're best at while you outsource the rest.

The Right Facilitator Matters More than You Think

Even if you have the resources to build this program internally, consider another limiting factor: Who do you have who can facilitate the material in a compelling way?

Being an effective facilitator of manager training is hard. Why? Here are five quick thoughts on what you need out of an instructor/facilitator:

» **The facilitator can't be a robot.** Great facilitators need to weave stories into the training if you're going to keep class interest and engagement high.[4]

» **Mechanics matter.** You'll have participant guides, slides, flip charts, videos, exercises and a bunch of other stuff. Something that sounds simple for facilitators to do—referencing page numbers from your materials so people don't get lost and otherwise spinning the program plates—is hard when everything's flying at one hundred mph.

» **Setting up and executing the exercises is hard.** You wouldn't think of this if you hadn't done it as much as I have. Your facilitator can't be cute on the exercises you have; they need to do basics, read the instructions, and be specific in the execution, because if you paraphrase what you want people to do, they get lost and it all goes to hell.

---

4. Thus, the biggest tradeoff you'll make as you try and identify an internal facilitator: do you use a good trainer who doesn't have background in managing people or go get a dynamic leader who hasn't trained before?

» **Pace, pace, pace.** Keeping your eye on the prize as an instructor is key. If you're doing a day of training and you get halfway through the day and you've only made it a quarter of the way through the material, you're in trouble. That's the norm, not the exception for most facilitators.

» **Conversations involving participants matter more than you covering material.** It's an art for how long to let the sharing and dialogue between classmates go on. Participation is key, disagreements amongst the attendees are gold. Great facilitators let them roll but keep their eye on the pace consideration mentioned earlier.

Bottom line: you need a subject matter expert who's comfortable with high degrees of chaos and ambiguity to facilitate your leadership/manager-of-people training. Plus, they have to be a bit of a performer in front of groups, be credible with the material (preferably having used the tools before), and be comfortable delivering a learning program.

This profile of the perfect facilitator is easy to outline, but hard to find in most companies.

Get to Your Final Version of the Training, Then Cut It by Half

If there's one thing I've learned in taking thousands of participants through manager training programs, it's that you almost always have too much material for the time budgeted when developing a module.

This problem is full of good intent, as the outline and materials you develop will be stocked with compelling things your managers should know.

Once you make your first run through the materials, cut the material by half for a better fit with the time budgeted. This formula/rule of thumb acknowledges that a great facilitator will draw conversations out of the managers in each session, and will seamlessly connect your attendees with concepts in a fluid fashion. But this organic and unplanned learning eats up time, and it's why most people never make it through their entire planned session the first time through.

Flip that premise around. If you didn't cut your materials and actually did make it all the way through, it's likely there was zero interaction between participants, the session was lame, the facilitator was below average, and there'll be no behavioral change as a result.

I know, I'm a ray of sunshine.[5] But these are facts based on my deep, hard-knock manager-training life experience.

Everyone Hates to Role Play, but Make It Nonnegotiable

Your participants won't want to role play as part of your sessions. They'll beg and potentially bribe you not to do it. You'll be tempted to skip this form of skill practice when pressed for time.

Don't give in. Role playing the skills you're covering in your manager training is critical and, in some ways, the only thing that really matters.

For anything related to manager training, role play in your session equals failure (the first repetition with any skill or tool you're using is the roughest), which is why no one wants to do it.

You've got to give them real practice using the skills you're teaching them. If they don't struggle initially in role play as a part of your training, there's ZERO chance they're going to try and use the skill in the real world.

To increase comfort with any skill, you should give your managers at least two to three repetitions with any skill, as they'll see the gradual improvement and be more likely to use the skill with their direct reports in the future.

---

5. When you're telling someone initial failure is likely, try saying, "I'm from corporate and I'm here to help" to break the tension. Sixty percent of the time it works every time.

If you don't force people to fail in your training, they'll never be effective in their real lives as managers.

Keep the Training Alive by Meeting to Talk about Real Life

Any training you conduct for your managers is only an event in time. You work hard to develop the training session, conduct it, perhaps send out a survey, and then presto! Everyone's back to their normal lives.

To keep conversations alive about the manager skills you're trying to sponsor and advocate for, a great idea is to meet once a month as a form of follow-up. The goal of these meetings should be to pre-announce the topic (a skill/tool you've already trained on), then ask all invited attendees to use the skill/tool in question (let's use coaching skills as an example) prior to the meeting.

Once you're in the meeting, you ask two or three individuals to share their experience using the skill/tool, focusing on the good, bad, and ugly, then facilitate a session where others can comment, assist, and encourage the brave soul who is serving as the case study.

As with the actual training session, the peer-based impromptu comments and conversations facilitated by you matter as much as the tool itself.

You're absolutely correct if you think this sounds like a self-help group with you as the armchair psychologist.[6]

Go help the people heal themselves!

---

6. Me: "My name is Kris." Group: "Hi Kris." Me: "It's been six days since I last avoided coaching an employee who needed it."

KD'S CHEAT SHEET
BUILDING A MANAGER/
LEADERSHIP TRAINING PROGRAM

DO THIS!

- Realize that as a leader of those who manage others, there's always room for your people managers to get better.
- Map out the ten most important conversations you'd like your managers of people to get better at as a guide for the program you want to build.
- Once mapped, determine if you can build it on your own or if you need to buy an outside program, or a hybrid approach.
- Always reserve time in your courses for skill practice/role play. It's the most important thing.
- Once you come up with your initial outline/content for any course, cut the content by half. You always develop more than you can execute initially.
- You'll need the time for great conversations between participants.

WATCH OUT FOR THESE TRAPS!

- Don't build courses around broad leadership content that has little to do with the areas your managers of people are struggling in ("Leaders Eat Last" versus "How do I get into this coaching conversation").
- Don't put a facilitator in to lead your training program who can't seamlessly manage the content you need to move through while allowing organic classroom conversations caused by great comments and questions from participants.
- Don't forget to keep the learning alive post-training by bringing your managers together once a month to talk about their challenges in using the skills with real employees.

RESOURCES FOR YOU ONLINE - BESTBOSSEVER.ORG

- Course outlines for the seven core courses included in this book: interviewing and selection, managing strengths and weaknesses, goal setting, coaching skills, change management, compensation, and performance management

 KRIS DUNN

The Superstars Are Never Who You Think They Are

Whenever I get a chance to lead a leadership/manager training class, I'm honored and humbled. *Honored* because the clients are great, the people are authentic, and we have a great day. *Humbled* because what managers have to do to be successful is incredibly hard.

As you might expect, we always do live practice on the skill/competency we're training on.

And there's always a simple but profound lesson present every time I get to train managers of people on any module covered in this book:

The stars are never who you think they are,
but they're right in front of you.

What do I mean by that? Simple. You expect the most experienced people in any manager training class to do the best in role play or skill practice. At times, that's true—but WOW—the most gratifying part of any training class I do is when a few of the more junior people in the class absolutely ROCK IT.

It almost always happens. There are always one or two junior people in every training class I do who are superstars related to the tools we're covering.

These less-experienced, often younger stars blow me away by displaying the following natural skills:

» **They're completely natural when it comes to stage banter and building trust/relationships.** They're fluid and weave what they're trying to get out of the employee session into a conversation that puts the person in front of them at ease.

» **They think on their feet.** Conversations with people who report to you are never easy. Employees object. They sidetrack you. They try to screw up your game. The stars I'm talking about have a natural ability to bring the conversation back to what's important. They don't get lost and the redirect never seems forced.

» **They are technically superior.** Got a coaching tool? Behavioral interviewing technique? Doing goal setting? These stars can memorize the outline of the tool, and they always make sure they get what they need—and more.

It happens so much it's *unexpected yet expected.* I go into the class saying to myself, "Okay, who's going to be the underdog out of this cast of characters who is going to outshine everyone else?"

If you've done managerial training and haven't seen this trend emerge, you're likely not doing enough skill practice/role play. Yes, they hate it and will cheer if you don't make them do it. But your adoption rate of the skills you're teaching drops by over 50 percent if you don't do skill practice/role play as part of your training.

You're hiding weak managers with elevated titles when you don't force them to show they can do the work you're covering in your manager training program.

The best part of doing leadership/manager training is the underdog star who emerges.

You're a superstar, kid. I hope your company realizes what they have. I know I've told them who you are.

22
Closing Time

You don't have to go home, but you can't stay here.
—Semisonic, "Closing Time"

We're at the end!

If you're a manager with a team of individual contributors, your job is to use the tools and cheat sheets included in *Best Boss Ever* to make small, sustainable improvements in the way you engage your team to get things done and encourage them to do the best work of their career.

In other words, go tear it up, kids.

But it's never that simple, right? For those of you who plowed all the way through this book or even power-browsed, it's easy to feel overwhelmed by the list of tools and life hacks for managers I've provided.

Breath deep. As *Scarface*'s Tony Montana would affirm, the world is yours.[1]

If You Found Two Things You'll Use in
This Book, You've Already Won

You don't need to deploy everything in this book next week. To make it big, start working on two areas until you master them, then add an additional two tools to your game when comfortable and ready.

---

1. For the uninitiated, Al Pacino played immigrant Tony in *Scarface*, with a key scene being the protagonist seeing a blimp with the words, "The World is Yours," which he took as a sign it was okay for him to have, uh, ambition.

Build your skills over time, and you win. But the journey doesn't start until you begin the experiment with your team.

Best Boss Ever has thirty-five tools and fourteen cheat sheets. You're unlikely to use all of it. Pick your favorites and start to use them this month. It will feel rough, forced, and unnatural, but once begun, it's half done. The first step is the most important, and you'll be at an expert level in no time as long as you keep getting repetitions with the tools you've selected.

Remember to Sound like You, Not Me

There's nothing worse than a person in authority getting super formal as they try to have an organic conversation with a direct report. Your employee's spidey sense goes up,[2] and the two-way interaction you want becomes almost impossible to achieve.

Being stiff decays trust. I want you to hit the steps/script in the tools provided, but it's just as important that you sound like you.

For best results, memorize rough outlines of the tools provided, and then insert your own personality as you deliver. Can you talk in your normal cadence/delivery, be informal,[3] but still manage to hit the broad steps or content in any of the tools we've provided?

That's the goal. Mix the technical aspects of the tool with your gift for gab and you're golden.

Remember that many of the tools presented in this book place a premium on employee participation. That reduces your burden to talk all the time, and as your employee speaks, you have some time to think about what's next on your end.

---

2. They often are concerned they're about to receive bad news, like they're being fired or perhaps Ted Lasso has been canceled.
3. Even meander a bit, but not so long that you lose your place in the tool in question. Art > Science.

Remember Your Employees Aren't Going to Know You Missed a Step

Here's something that should make you feel better about using the tools in this book:

> Your employees are never going to know that you "screwed up" when using any tool or hack from *Best Boss Ever*.

Let's say you're trying the Six-Step Coaching Tool and totally whiffed on Step #3. You feel the burn and acknowledge what you missed in your mind as you finish your delivery of Step #4.

Guess what? The employee in front of you has no clue. To them, it just seems like you've slowed down and are more intent to have a directed, meaningful conversation than usual. Unless you visibly fold or shut down because of the skipped step, you're still in great shape.

Complete the conversation, and do a two-minute postmortem about what you missed for future reference. Nobody dies when you screw it up. You're still outperforming 90 percent of your manager-of-people peers by using one of the tools provided.

The Most Important Thing Is for You to Become a Career Agent

Most of the tools in the book are designed to help you have better conversations with your direct reports. The vibe to most of these conversations is how you can help the employees on your team do the best work of their careers.

For best results after finishing this book, go reread Chapter 4 (Becoming a Career Agent Is the Obvious Play). In that chapter, you'll find the following definition of what I've defined as a Career Agent:

A boss/manager of people who is a *Career Agent* is there to get the job done and get business results, but they'll accomplish something very important along the way. A Career Agent, as a manager of people, approaches every assignment to the team, every task, and all feedback through a simple lens related to the team member/employee in question:

What's in it for you to do what I'm asking you to do?

This chapter captures the opportunity for all of us who lead teams. If we make developing the talent around us (regardless of career stage or current performance level) the first priority, results always follow.

If you want engagement, retention, and accolades as a manager of people, become a Career Agent for those who report to you.

Go do great things.

—KD out

23
Tribute

This is ten percent luck, twenty percent skill
Fifteen percent concentrated power of will
Five percent pleasure, fifty percent pain
And a hundred percent reason to remember the name.
—Fort Minor

I didn't just roll out of bed with a nonspecific undergraduate degree as someone with fully formed opinions on how to be a manager of people. Like many of you, I had role models along the way who led and mentored by example. Here is a roster of the bosses who taught me how to push people for more in an authentic, transparent way.

Pour one out for these all-time greats who have all risen to the level of Best Boss Ever for many through the years with their own unique style and grace:

Shannon Russo

Ty Breland

Scott Stone

Lisa Bryant

Don Sykes

Marilyn Brooks

Todd Gurley

Thanks to these giants, without whom I would have achieved little. I owe you and think about what you taught me often.

Index